Attack at Daylight and Whip Them

THE BATTLE OF SHILOH, APRIL 6-7, 1862

by Gregory A. Mertz

EMERGING CIVIL WAR SERIES

Chris Mackowski, series editor
Chris Kolakowski, chief historian

The Emerging Civil War Series

offers compelling, easy-to-read overviews of some of the Civil War's most important battles and stories.

Recipient of the Army Historical Foundation's Lieutenant General Richard G. Trefry Award for contributions to the literature on the history of the U.S. Army

Also part of the Emerging Civil War Series:

The Aftermath of Battle: The Burial of the Civil War Dead by Meg Groeling

All the Fighting They Want: The Atlanta Campaign, from Peachtree Creek to the Surrender of the City, July 18-September 2, 1864 by Stephen Davis

All Hell Can't Stop Them: The Battles for Chattanooga: Missionary Ridge and Ringgold, November 24-27, 1863 by David A. Powell

Battle Above the Clouds: Lifting the Siege of Chattanooga and the Battle of Lookout Mountain, October 16-November 24, 1863 by David A. Powell

Bushwhacking on a Grand Scale: The Battle of Chickamauga, Sept. 18-20, 1863 by William Lee White

Let us Die Like Men: The Battle of Franklin, Nov. 30, 1864 by William Lee White

A Long and Bloody Task: The Atlanta Campaign, from Dalton to Kennesaw to the Chattahooche, May 5-July 18, 1864 by Stephen Davis

Richmond Shall Not Be Given Up: The Seven Days' Battles, June 25-July 1, 1862 by Doug Crenshaw

That Field of Blood: The Battle of Antietam, September 17, 1862 by Daniel J. Vermilya

For a complete list of titles in the Emerging Civil War Series, visit www.emergingcivilwar.com.

THE BATTLE OF SHILOH,
APRIL 6-7, 1862

by Gregory A. Mertz

EMERGING CIVIL WAR SERIES

SB

Savas Beatie

California

First edition, first printing

ISBN-13 (paperback): 978-1-61121-313-3
ISBN-13 (ebook): 978-161121-314-0

Library of Congress Cataloging-in-Publication Data

Names: Mertz, Gregory A., author.
Title: Attack at daylight and whip them: the Battle of Shiloh, April 6-7, 1862 / by Gregory A. Mertz.
Description: El Dorado Hills, California : Savas Beatie, [2019]
Identifiers: LCCN 2018021804| ISBN 9781611213133 (pbk : alk. paper) | ISBN 9781611213140 (ebk)
Subjects: LCSH: Shiloh, Battle of, Tenn., 1862. | Shiloh National Military Park (Tenn. and Miss.)--Guidebooks.
Classification: LCC E473.54 .M47 2018 | DDC 973.7/31--dc23
LC record available at https://lccn.loc.gov/2018021804

Published by
Savas Beatie LLC
989 Governor Drive, Suite 102
El Dorado Hills, California 95762
Phone: 916-941-6896
Email: sales@savasbeatie.com
Web: www.savasbeatie.com

Savas Beatie titles are available at special discounts for bulk purchases in the United States by corporations, institutions, and other organizations. For more details, please contact Special Sales, 989 Governor Drive, Ste 102, El Dorado Hills, CA 95762, or you may e-mail us at sales@savasbeatie.com, or visit our website at www.savasbeatie.com for additional information.

To the memory and honor of the Nickel sisters:
Edna Mertz, Verna Beinke, Marie Parker, Helen Fink, Dorothy Ruby,
Betty Mertz (my mother), and Lillian Putnam—an amazing group of role models
to the entire extended family, whose strength comes from walking with the Lord

Table of Contents

ABOVE and **OPPOSITE:** Two figures—an officer and a cavalryman—from the Confederate memorial. For an explanation of their symbolic significance, see Chapter Two. (gam)(gam)

For the Emerging Civil War Series

Theodore P. Savas, *publisher*
Chris Mackowski, *series editor*
Christopher Kolakowski, *chief historian*
Sarah Keeney, *editorial consultant*
Kristopher D. White, *co-founding editor*

Maps by Hal Jespersen
Design and layout by Chris Mackowski

List of Maps

Maps by Hal Jespersen

The largest of the known Confederate burial trenches, near the Water Oaks Pond and the Crossroads of the Corinth and Hamburg-Purdy Road, is indicative of the heavy casualties that fell on both days of the battle in this vicinity. It is one of five Confederate burial trenches marked within the park. (gam)

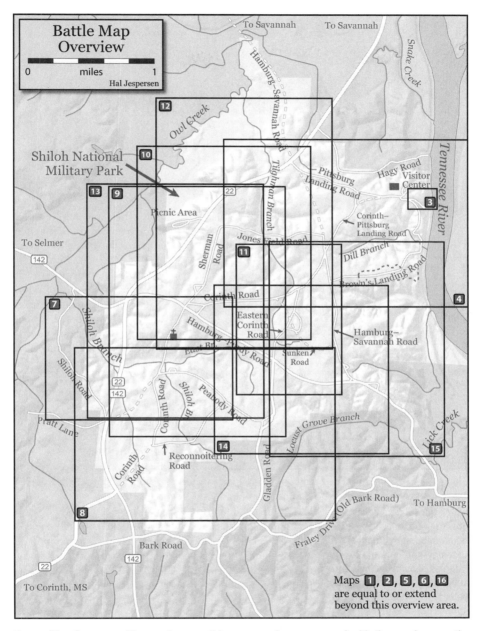

Battle Map Overview

0   miles   1

Hal Jespersen

To Savannah   To Savannah

12

Shiloh National Military Park

10

Owl Creek

Snake Creek

Hamburg–Savannah Road

Tilghman Branch

Pittsburg Landing Road

Hagy Road

Visitor Center

3

Tennessee River

13   9

Picnic Area

22

To Selmer

142

Sherman Road

Jones Field Road

11

Corinth– Pittsburg Landing Road

Dill Branch

Brown's Landing Road

7

Corinth Road

Eastern Corinth Road

Hamburg– Savannah Road

4

Shiloh Branch

Hamburg–Purdy Road

East Br.

Sunken Road

Shiloh Road

22

142

Corinth Road

Shiloh Br.

Peabody Road

Locust Grove Branch

Lick Creek

Pratt Lane

15

Corinth Road

Reconnoitering Road

Gladden Road

14

8

Fraley Drive (Old Bark Road)

To Hamburg

Bark Road

22

142

To Corinth, MS

Maps 1, 2, 5, 6, 16 are equal to or extend beyond this overview area.

BATTLE MAP OVERVIEW—The numbers on this map overlay correspond with the numbers on the detailed maps within the book. Use this map to determine where any of the detailed maps would fit onto the overall Shiloh battlefield landscape.

✏️ Acknowledgments

My many visits to Shiloh as a boy were the result of being a member of Boy Scout Troop 782 from Ellisville, Missouri, and the trek it made to the battlefield every spring. One of the profound, impactful moments I still recall occurred when riding through the battlefield during one of those outings. The driver was one of my favorite adult scout leaders, Bill Hess, and I asked him whether our route would take us past the "long row of cannon," or words to that effect. Mr. Hess knew exactly what I meant and said that it would. One of my youth leaders, Jody Bearden, also responded to

About midnight of April 6, 1862, a driving rainstorm pelted the soldiers several hours after a massive bombardment by Ruggles' Battery. After the war, Daniel Ruggles became an inventor, submitting several rainmaking patents that included the application of explosives. Perhaps Ruggles associated the downpour at Shiloh with the artillery fire he directed, and his experiences at Shiloh may have contributed to his rainmaking ideas. (gam)

my question albeit in a tone of disgust: "It's called 'Ruggles' Battery,'" rebuffed Jody.

With the help of a stinging nudge from Jody, I made an important transition from simply being impressed with a huge collection of artillery pieces and numerous monuments at Shiloh to truly understanding what happened during the battle and during the Civil War as a whole. The end result has been a career as a historian with the National Park Service that has spanned more than three decades. So, the first acknowledgment is to Jody, then extends to the other leaders and members of the troop who were such an important part of my formative years.

Others continued to play important roles in furthering my desire to explore more deeply into the battle. I was thrilled when Wiley Sword wrote his classic *Shiloh: Bloody April* and when I got him to sign my copy of his book on my honeymoon (my wife, Diane, and I met on a Civil War tour

The grave of Daniel Ruggles in the Fredericksburg, Virginia, Confederate Cemetery is only one mile from where the author has had an office for some 25 years. The author's interest in the Civil War always seems to have Ruggles associated with it somehow. (gam)

conducted by Ed Bearss, and we included another tour with Ed as part of our honeymoon).

I have a tremendous amount of respect for Tim Smith and all of his insightful writings on Shiloh. I was exceedingly fortunate to participate in a tour of Shiloh led by Tim and Ed Bearss as I neared the end of this project.

The afternoon that I read the chapter in Confederates in the Attic about Tony Horwitz's conversation with Stacy Allen was nothing short of eye opening. Stacy's own writings and his suggestions with this project are much appreciated.

My friend and colleague Frank O'Reilly insisted that I attend the Shiloh 150th anniversary and accompanied me to it; thanks for being an inspiration, a motivator, and a friend. The 150th guides—Jeff Gentsch, Bjorn Skaptason, Charlie Spearman, and Chris Mekow—sparked a resurgence in my delving back into Shiloh.

Thanks to Chris Mackowski and Kris White with Emerging Civil War. Everyone who knows me in the context of the Civil War knows that Shiloh holds a special place in my heart, and I am so thrilled that they thought of me to write the volume for this amazing battle in their impressive series.

PHOTO CREDITS:
Alabama Department of Archives and History (adah); *Battles and Leaders of the Civil War* (bl); *Civil War in Kentucky: Battle for the Bluegrass* (cwk); *History of the Orphan Brigade* (hoob); Library of Congress (loc); London Stereoscopic & Photographic Company (lspc); Louisiana State University (lsu); Chris Mackowski (cm); Greg Mertz (gam); Diane Mertz (sdm); National Archives (na); National Park Service (nps); State Library of Louisiana (sll); U.S. Military Institute (usmi); University of Kentucky Townsend Collection (uktc); Wilson's Creek National Battlefield (wcnb)

Touring the Battlefield

While this book will attempt to tell the battle as chronologically as possible, it is also a guidebook designed to take the reader through the battlefield, taking in the terrain. The battlefield tour will generally follow along the National Park Service driving tour route with some additional stops, along with a couple of detours.

Because it is not possible to follow a purely chronological tour, you are highly encouraged to begin your tour at the visitor center, there utilizing the exhibits and the movie to gain an overview of the battle before taking the tour.

At the visitor center and again at one of the first tour stops for Grant's Last Line are identical plaques labeled "Explanatory" that will be extremely helpful to examine. Just by looking at the markers, visitors can determine the basics of what the color, shape, and orientation of each represents.

You will find the battlefield full of monuments not included on the tour that you may wish to visit. When that occurs, it is permissible to park on the road shoulders. Pull off the road far enough to open the doors of your vehicle without the door protruding into the roadway.

The presence of crops at different times of the year may impact your understanding of what happened in some of the fields. The heat of warm months may cause you to seek shade near the tour stops when reading the narrative, rather than standing right where the tour directs you to stand.

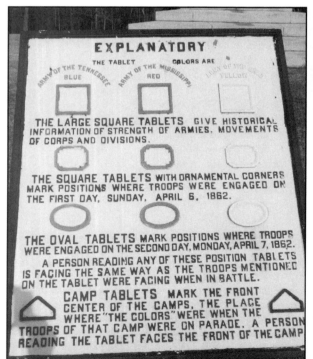

Many stops along this tour will utilize the park's orientation stations, with concrete pads and a wayside marker usually featuring a map showing your location relative to the action, and a brief narrative summarizing the significance of the site. (gam)

The shape, color and orientation of each tablet automatically inform visitors whether it describes actions of the first or second day of the battle, to which army the unit belonged, and which direction the unit faced. (gam)

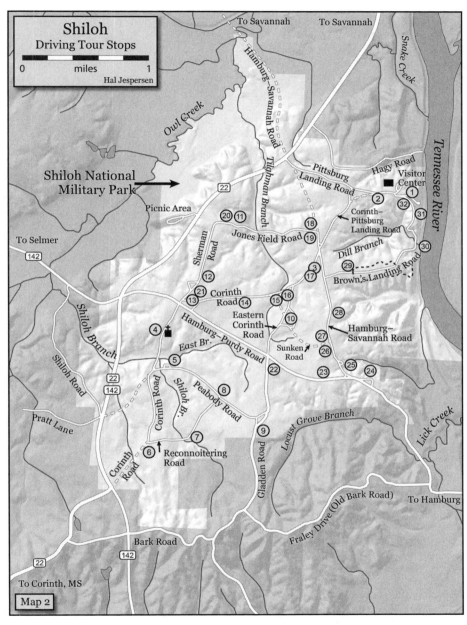

SHILOH DRIVING TOUR STOPS—Though the driving tour for this book closely follows the park driving tour, it will make some significant detours, and the numbering system for the tour stops is completely different from that of the park self-guided tour.

Foreword

BY TIMOTHY B. SMITH

Shiloh is a special place. Some say it is mystical, others that it merely resounds in historical ambiance. It is a place of past horror, while abounding in pleasure today. It is complex yet simple in its beauty. It was once a place of upheaval, but today it is tranquil. It is finally a place of peace.

Many in the past have noted Shiloh's beauty and reverence. One of the battle's veterans, later a Confederate general, Francis Shoup, years afterward remarked in reference to the blooming of dogwoods there in the spring, "I never see them now that I do not think of Shiloh." Decades later, historian Thomas L. Connelly warmly remembered "the balmy summer nights when my brothers and I slipped onto the old battleground at Shiloh, half afraid of the young park rangers with their new Pershing hats and well-thumbed park guidebooks, and half fearful of the ghosts of the 23,000 casualties who everyone said roamed the field by night." As a former "young park ranger," I can attest to the feeling of that mystique. For several years I had the privilege of living on the battlefield itself, and although I never saw or felt anything that would even remotely lead me to believe there was any kind of paranormal activity there, I always felt a definite aura of enchantment, of being in the figurative presence of the veterans who had fought there.

Few can tread Shiloh's historic fields today without coming away with this feeling of mystique. One has only to watch the slow but steady current of the magnificent Tennessee River at Pittsburg Landing to understand what was at stake there in April 1862, perhaps even the development of a great nation itself. Bloody Pond offers visitors the chance today to ponder the human toll of the fighting, even while perhaps literally reflecting in its tranquil waters. Shiloh Church to this day relates the contradiction of religion and morality nestled amid such non-religious activities as killing and hatred. And the icons that the Hornet's Nest and Sunken Road have become give visitors the opportunity to put themselves, via their imaginations,

While the face of the wounded soldier on the Tennessee monument reveals his weariness and waning consciousness, he has enough awareness to muster what strength he can to grasp the folds of the battleflag and lift it off the ground as a colorbearer (whose hand holding the staff is visible) kneels over to help the fallen comrade. (cm)

The stream-side glen where Albert Sidney Johnston died provides a peaceful atmosphere for contemplation. (cm)

back in the midst of the fighting—even if only for a fleeting moment. All battlefields are important in their own right, but there is something special about Shiloh.

As important as a pilgrimage to today's battlefield of Shiloh is to many, the results of that battle are even more important. As the first major action of the war, one which produced tens of thousands of casualties, Shiloh was a collective blow to all Americans when the casualty figures became known. The sheer enormity of the dead and wounded told Americans that they had stumbled into something that would forever change their nation and their lives.

In a more strategic sense, Shiloh was also one of the few truly war-altering episodes of the conflict, ranking it with the likes of Antietam, Gettysburg, Vicksburg, and Chickamauga. For the Federals, the victory at Shiloh eventually would loom as the greatest triumph in terms of numbers within the Mississippi Valley campaign. While not even on the great Father of Waters but on a tributary of a tributary, Shiloh was nevertheless one of the major steppingstones to Union victory in the valley, in the west itself, and indeed in the entire war.

On the other hand, the loss at Shiloh was a major setback for the Confederates. In what was literally a do-or-die situation that Confederate commander Albert Sidney Johnston labeled as time to "conquer or perish," Shiloh marked the best chance the South had to defend its critical railroads at Corinth, Mississippi, and to throw back the Union advance southward against the cotton states. At no other time would the South have the opportunity to meet and defeat an enemy army with so much at stake and under such equal odds.

Yet the fighting at Shiloh, particularly the loss for the South, also brought new problems over and above the massive casualties and the eventual loss of Corinth and its railroads. Shiloh affected Confederate ability to wage war in the West for the rest of the conflict. The loss of Albert Sidney Johnston was especially important. Many historians have argued for or against Johnston's ability, but no one will ever know for sure because of his premature death on April 6, 1862. The plain truth, however, was that with Johnston's loss at Shiloh, his perishing in this attempt to conquer, Confederate command in the West was left for the remainder of the war in a state of turmoil. Certainly, another full general, P. G. T. Beauregard, did take over for Johnston on the battlefield itself and for a while afterwards in the defense of Corinth, but Beauregard was an administration enemy who could never garner enough confidence from Jefferson Davis to remain in command long. The same was true of Joseph E. Johnston, and indeed both held only short periods of field command in the West, mere months each. That left most of the war in the West to be led by a tier of generals lower than the original full generals, many who were actually peers or near equals in corps command at Shiloh. With Johnston's death, the Confederacy lost the only available full general who had Davis's approval, leaving the four corps commanders at Shiloh (and their supporters) to battle among themselves for status and command authority for the rest of the war. The resulting chaos between William J. Hardee, Braxton Bragg, Leonidas Polk, and John C. Breckinridge, all peers at Shiloh, left the Confederate West in turmoil.

A Dahlgren cannon overlooks Pittsburg Landing from the National Cemetery. Union Gen. William T. Sherman first surveyed Pittsburg Landing from this area when the river was swollen due to excessive rain, and he was impressed that even in high water the landing could accommodate boats. (gam)

Shiloh was thus truly important, so it is fitting that today such a mystical place is preserved as one of our national parks. And, the benefits are numerous. The importance of preservation is on full display as the battlefield itself is perhaps the best source historians now have to study the fighting there. The patriotism unleashed when coming under the spell of Shiloh also teaches each new generation its history and what it can achieve in the future.

There are numerous ways to tour and explore the battlefield at Shiloh, but historian Greg Mertz, in this book, has provided a wonderfully thorough and comprehensive tour guide that will educate the Shiloh pilgrim about this truly amazing example of American combat. Whether reading these pages at home while planning a trip to the battlefield or on the field itself, *Attack at Daylight and Whip Them* provides a magnificent initiation to the battlefield, as well as to the engrossing experience that is the Shiloh mystique.

Award-winning historian TIMOTHY B. SMITH *teaches history at the University of Tennessee at Martin. He has written more than a dozen books and is a former park ranger at Shiloh National Military Park.*

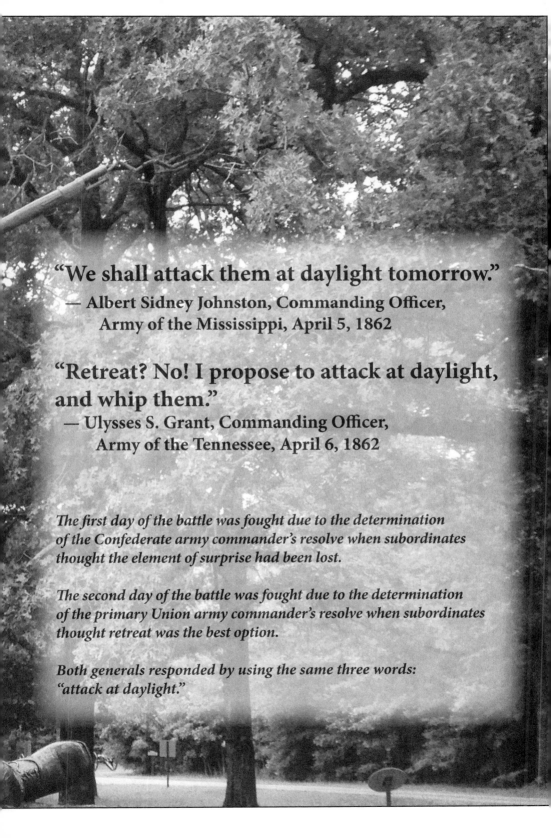

"We shall attack them at daylight tomorrow."
— Albert Sidney Johnston, Commanding Officer,
   Army of the Mississippi, April 5, 1862

"Retreat? No! I propose to attack at daylight, and whip them."
— Ulysses S. Grant, Commanding Officer,
   Army of the Tennessee, April 6, 1862

The first day of the battle was fought due to the determination of the Confederate army commander's resolve when subordinates thought the element of surprise had been lost.

The second day of the battle was fought due to the determination of the primary Union army commander's resolve when subordinates thought retreat was the best option.

Both generals responded by using the same three words: "attack at daylight."

The Campaign

CHAPTER ONE

April 6-7, 1862

A bronze eagle with a fifteen-foot wingspan is perched on a globe atop a 75-foot high column on the tallest monument to grace the Shiloh battlefield: the Iowa monument. By war's end 67,000 Iowa soldiers volunteered to enlist—the greatest percentage of men to volunteer than from any state, north or south. (cm)

Tensions were high in the fall of 1860 when Abraham Lincoln was elected the sixteenth president of the United States. Lincoln's platform that slavery should not be permitted to extend into the U.S. territories was intolerable to the people of seven slave-holding states of the Deep South, which decided to leave the country and form the Confederate States of America.

Most in the North felt that the distinctive form of government that the Founding Fathers molded should not be placed in jeopardy. Being allowed to have a voice in government was a precious right, and a group of people should not be allowed to destroy that country just because the policies of the land were not to their liking.

Civil War erupted at Fort Sumter in Charleston, South Carolina, on April 12, 1861. Three days later, Lincoln responded by putting out a call for 75,000 troops from the remaining states in the Union to put down the rebellion. With the outbreak of war, four slave states that had previously decided to stay with the Union now decided that they would join with the other seven states rather than send their sons to Lincoln's army to force the seceded states to return to the Union.

Tennessee was one such state to leave the Union at this juncture, and the decision would be particularly fateful. Of the 10,455 military actions that officially comprised the American Civil War, Tennessee hosted 1,462 battles and other engagements. Virginia was the only state to witness more fighting than Tennessee.

The first major land battle of the war was fought on July 21, 1861, near a railroad junction at Manassas, Virginia, and along the banks of a stream named Bull Run. It was the largest battle fought thus far in all of American history. With some 900 dead and another 3,000 wounded

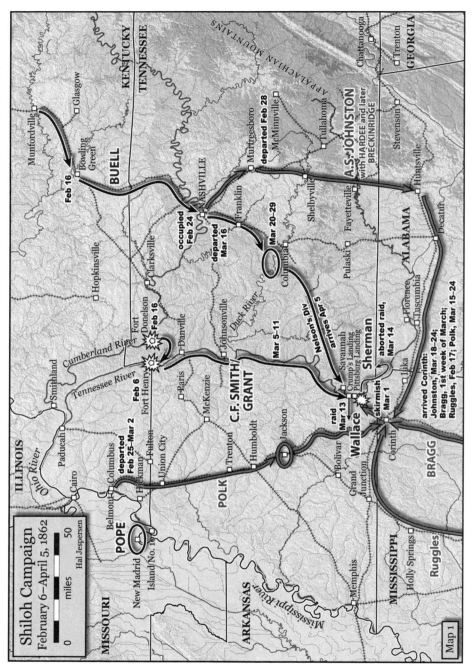

THE SHILOH CAMPAIGN—Union success at Forts Henry and Donelson in February 1862 allow Union forces to use the Tennessee River as an avenue of advance deep into the heart of Tennessee. As Confederate forces concentrate at Corinth, Mississippi, Union forces threaten rail lines leading into Corinth in March 1862. Union forces plan for the Army of the Ohio under D. C. Buell to join U. S. Grant camped near Shiloh Church for a joint thrust on Corinth.

on both sides—Americans all—the battle alerted the people of both North and South that this would not be a relatively bloodless, one-battle war as many of them had imagined. What the First Battle of Manassas, or Bull Run, failed to do, however, was to illuminate just *how* costly the human toll of the Civil War would be. Light shone on that cost eight months later—at Shiloh.

The April 6-7, 1862, battle of Shiloh witnessed *five times* as many casualties as Manassas. Officially, 3,482 were killed, 16,420 were wounded, and 3,844 were reported as missing— many of whom were captured. Shiloh had become the bloodiest battle in American history. The casualty count seemed to astonish the population like no other battle of the Civil War. Subsequent, more-brutal battles in terms of casualties would continue to stir emotions of sadness and anger in the people of the North and South, but even so, probably no other battle shocked and stunned the populace as Shiloh had done.

As one Southern writer purportedly said, "The South never smiled again after Shiloh."

*   *   *

Rivers, roads and railroads—these features often dictated where and why battles were fought. The reason a battle was fought at Shiloh can be simply stated after looking at these three types of transportation routes. The Tennessee River provided the Union army with an avenue of advance to adjacent Pittsburg Landing. The Confederates responded to the Union excursion down the Tennessee by concentrating their forces via rail at a railroad junction in Corinth, Mississippi, 22 miles to the south. The Corinth Road linked the landing with the rail junction. Battle erupted along the Corinth Road, three miles away from the river landing, near a simple Methodist church named "Shiloh Meeting House."

Rivers also dominated the larger strategy as well. Three important rivers in the western states of the Confederacy have north-south channels, which were very inviting passages of advance for Union troops—the Mississippi River, the Tennessee River, and a portion of the Cumberland River.

Most prominent of all was the Mississippi. Historian James M. McPherson did not overstate the vulnerability

The Tennessee River was navigable from its mouth, where it flows into the Ohio River, all the way to a bridge at Florence, Alabama. The other major Confederate army in the field, operating predominantly in Virginia, did not face the challenge of Union waterway invasion routes. The rivers between the opposing capitals of Washington, D.C., and Richmond, Virginia, flowed west to east and formed obstacles to the advance of Union troops. (gam)

In the aftermath of the victory at Fort Donelson, 48-year-old Henry Halleck had a falling out with his successful subordinate, Grant, and turned command of the army over to Gen. Charles Smith on March 4, 1862—just a month before the battle of Shiloh. (na)

Earning the nickname of "Unconditional Surrender" Grant because the terms he offered for the capitulation of Fort Donelson matched his initials, a puzzled 39-year-old Ulysses S. Grant did not understand why Halleck relieved him. (loc)

the Mississippi River imposed upon the Confederacy when he wrote that it was "an arrow thrust into the heart of the Lower South." The struggles by the Confederates to defend the north-south rivers flowing through or bordering Tennessee were further complicated by the superiority of the Federal navy over the fledgling Confederate navy.

With the Confederacy logically constructing defenses along various points of the all-important Mississippi, Union forces sidestepped those strongholds and made their first major thrusts in the western theater of the Civil War on the waters of the Tennessee and Cumberland Rivers. Union Gen. Ulysses S. Grant, supported by the U.S. Navy, easily defeated and captured Fort Henry on the Tennessee River, 100 miles north of Pittsburg Landing, on February 6, 1862. Grant then turned to the Cumberland River and its primary defense at Fort Donelson, just twelve miles east of Fort Henry. There, Grant achieved a huge victory with the surrender of some 12,000 Confederates on February 16. With the garrison at Fort Donelson no longer a threat to the rear of Union operations on the Tennessee River, Grant turned his attention back to that river. He established his headquarters at Savannah, Tennessee, about nine miles north of Pittsburg Landing.

The Union plan for the spring of 1862 was simple and logical. The Confederate build-up at Corinth would be their target. Grant, with an army of about 48,000 men that came to be known as the "Army of the Tennessee," was to await the arrival of a second Union force comprised of 37,000 troops, the Army of the Ohio, under Gen. Don Carlos Buell. Together, under department commander Maj. Gen. Henry W. Halleck, they planned to proceed to Corinth to defeat the outnumbered Confederates.

Grant was under strict orders to avoid a fight until the arrival of Buell, but he did not stand by idly waiting the juncture of the two forces. Grant's troops attempted raids on the railroad lines feeding into Corinth. One of Grant's six divisions, numbering 7,500 soldiers under Gen. Lew Wallace, disembarked at Crump's Landing, six miles north of Pittsburg Landing. Wallace ventured west on March 13 and disrupted the Mobile and Ohio Railroad—the north-south line that passed through Corinth. The next day, Brig. Gen. William T. Sherman's division on army transports on the Tennessee River bypassed Pittsburg Landing; adverse weather, however, hampered its effort to damage the east-west Memphis and Charleston Railroad at points east of Corinth.

During this expedition, Sherman's naval escort pointed out that a Confederate force had fired upon the gunboats from a hill during an earlier waterborne reconnaissance on March 1. (On this same hill now stands the National Cemetery.) A concerned Sherman suggested that some Union forces occupy the area to prevent Confederates from reappearing and threatening operations south of Pittsburg Landing. Sherman's subsequent inspection of the area resulted in his assessment that it was an excellent site for a camp and soon all of the army, except for Lew Wallace's command, was dispersed west of Pittsburg Landing, poised for the campaign against Corinth as soon as Buell arrived.

The Confederate army at Corinth, under Gen. Albert Sidney Johnston, did not intend to allow the Union armies to assemble an overwhelming force at Pittsburg Landing. Johnston, with nearly 45,000 men, planned to attack and destroy Grant's force of 40,000 at Shiloh before the juncture with Buell's army could take place.

As Sherman examined the area where the troops might bivouac, one of his concerns was whether the ground was defensible. To the north flowed Owl and Snake creeks, and to the south flowed Lick Creek, and even when not at flood stage, they were barriers to an enemy attack, protecting the sides or the flanks of the army. About four miles out, the army could be positioned behind another set of streams, Shiloh Branch (a tributary of Owl Creek) and Locust Grove Branch (a tributary of Lick Creek), which provided some degree of protection along the front of the army.

Grant had a field headquarters above the landing, but he spent his evenings in Savannah, staying in the Cherry Mansion. Buell would be arriving via Savannah, and Grant wanted to consult with him there.

Cannon fire interrupted Grant's breakfast on the morning of April 6, 1862. Soon Grant and his staff were off for the steamer *Tigress* to determine which portion of his army as under attack. As they neared Crump's Landing

TOP: Grant headquartered in Savannah—marked today by a monument—instead of with his army at Pittsburg Landing because Buell was to arrive via Savannah. Unbeknownst to Grant, Buell had arrived on April 5, but felt no sense of urgency to meet with him. Before the two could consult on the following day, disturbing battle sounds from the south dramatically altered the day's plan. (sdm)

BOTTOM: On the morning of April 6, Grant was sitting at the breakfast table of Annie Irwin Cherry when cannon fire from the south became audible. "Holding, untasted, a cup of coffee," Mrs. Cherry remembered, "he paused in conversation to listen a moment at the report of another cannon." (gam)

it became obvious that Lew Wallace's isolated division was not the target. The *Tigress* steamed on to Pittsburg Landing, where it docked about 8:30 a.m.

As the plank was laid out from the *Tigress* to the landing, Capt. John A. Rawlins of Grant's staff met the general and provided an assessment of the fight—"the attack was a general one, all along the line." Grant's first response was to order Wallace to bring his troops to the main army.

One of the new units that had just arrived that morning and was still at the landing was the 15th Iowa under Col. Hugh

The U.S.S. *Tigress*, Grant's flagship, is the second boat from the right. It sank trying to run past the Vicksburg, Mississippi, batteries in 1863. At Shiloh, on April 6, late in the afternoon, the Confederate army neared Pittsburg Landing and shells began to land where the steamboats were moored. "The steamboat 'Rocket,' loaded with ammunition, started at full speed down the river," noted Capt. Douglas Putnam, Jr., a volunteer aid of Grant. (bl)

T. Reid. Someone instructed the colonel: "After the men have had their coffee and received ammunition, to move to the top of the bluff and stop all stragglers and await further orders." The person issuing the instructions added, "I am General Grant."

The lack of urgency in getting the 15th Iowa into position to halt shirkers is evidence that the situation at Pittsburg Landing was still reasonably composed at that moment. All would change relatively soon.

The commanding general had ammunition sent to the battlefront and then rode off with his staff to see the situation for himself. "We met hundreds of cowardly renegades fleeing to the river and reporting their regiments cut to pieces," grumbled Capt. W. S. Hillyer of Grant's staff. Grant was "[c]ool and undismayed as ever," Hillyer observed, and "the General issued orders and sent his aides flying over the field."

As evening neared and the chaos at the landing was likely at its worst, the vanguard of Buell's army, a division under Brig. Gen. William Nelson arrived. The 300-pound former naval officer had the nickname of "Bull" and a gruff personality to match. Nelson himself came over in the first boat conveying his men across the river. The large general jumped his horse out of the boat, "drew his sword and rode right into the crowd of refugees," according to John A. Cockerill, a musician in the 24th Ohio, who said the general hollered, "If you won't fight, get out of the way, and let men come here who will!"

Of the reinforcements rushing to the battlefield, most did not make it in time to join in the first day's fight. However, even though April 6, 1862, had been a rough day for Grant, his army had held on to Pittsburg Landing and his confidence remained high.

*   *   *

The night of April 6-7 was a miserable night for the for the Union army commander, though. Just 48 hours earlier, Grant's horse had slipped and fallen while going down the steep bank leading down to Pittsburg Landing. On the night after the first day of the battle, Grant recalled, "My ankle was so much swollen from the fall of my horse the Friday night preceding, and the bruise was so painful, that I could get no rest."

In addition to his physical discomfort, the elements did not cooperate: a torrential rain started about midnight. Grant concluded that "[t]he drenching rain would have precluded the possibility of sleep." He tried to escape the rain by going to the log-house at the top of the hill that had been his Pittsburg Landing headquarters, but he found that had been taken over as a field hospital. "The sight was more unendurable than encountering the enemy's fire," wrote Grant, "and I returned to my tree in the rain."

Under or near his headquarters tree, Grant had several conversations that demonstrated his lack of concern about the outcome of the first day's battle. His troops had repelled the final attack of the day, and with reinforcements now on hand, he was confident that the outcome of the second day's battle would be favorable.

Buell arrived at Pittsburg Landing about an hour ahead of the lead elements of his Army of the Ohio. The thousands of stragglers and chaos at the landing apparently convinced him that Grant's army was in the grips of a catastrophe. Rawlins indicated that Buell asked, "What preparations have you made for retreating?" and that Grant replied, "I have not despaired of whipping them, general." Buell later called the account, "ridiculous and absurd," but other witnesses report Buell uneasy about the situation. "Buell seemed to mistrust us," Sherman recalled, "and repeatedly said that he did not like the looks of things, especially about the boat-landing, and I really feared he would not cross over his army that night, lest he should become involved in our general disaster."

Even some of Grant's loyal staff and subordinates thought retreat to be prudent considering the situation facing the army. Grant's engineer Col. James B. McPherson asked Grant, "Shall I make preparation for a retreat?"

Cannon just outside the walls of the National Cemetery mark Grant's Last Line. "I remember well seeing a mounted officer carrying a United States flag," wrote Douglas Putnam, "riding back and forth on top of the bank, pleading and entreating. . . . 'Men for God's sake, for your country's sake, for your own sake, come up here, form a line, and make one more stand.'" But Putnam observed that "the only reply I heard was some one saying, 'That man talks well, don't he?'" (gam)

Though the 37-year-old William "Bull" Nelson was promoted to major general three months after Shiloh, he suffered one of the most lopsided Union defeats of the entire war as an independent commander of a 6,850 man force in the August 29-30, 1862, battle of Richmond, Kentucky. The next month, he let his temper get away from him by slapping the face of fellow Union General Jefferson C. Davis, who promptly shot and killed Nelson. (loc)

CENTERFOLD: As evening neared and the chaos at the landing was likely at its worst, the vanguard of Buell's army arrived—men of Nelson's division. "Thousands of panic-stricken wretches swarmed from the river's edge far up toward the top of the steep," one of Buell's soldiers observed, "a heaving, surging herd of humanity, smitten with a very frenzy of fright and despair." (loc)

"Retreat? No!" the commanding general emphatically responded. "I propose to attack at daylight, and whip them."

Sherman was of like mind with McPherson. "The only thing just then possible, as it seemed to me," Sherman later told a reporter, "was to put the river between us and the enemy and recuperate."

But just before he nearly expressed this pessimistic view to Grant, he suddenly decided to start the conversation differently. "Well, Grant," Sherman began, "we've had the devil's own day, haven't we?"

"Yes," Grant admitted, "lick 'em to-morrow, though."

That determination was one of the key reasons why Grant would come to be regarded as a great general. Whether Grant was up against questionable political generals or talented professional military leaders, or whether facing green inexperienced troops or hardened veterans, his resolve was the same. Sherman recalled that Grant "ordered me to be ready to assume the offensive in the

A graduate of the West Point class of 1841, which furnished twenty generals to the Civil War, the 44-year-old Don Carlos Buell had been assigned to advance his Army of the Ohio into East Tennessee. Since that region lacked adequate roads and railroads to move and supply a sizeable army, Buell recommended a movement utilizing the Cumberland and Tennessee Rivers as routes of invasion instead. (loc)

morning, saying that, as he had observed at Fort Donelson at the crisis of the battle, both sides seemed defeated, and whoever assumed the offensive was sure to win."

In the aftermath of the surprise at Shiloh, Grant once again faced cynicism. Though Grant had not been defeated at Shiloh, criticism of the manner in which he won the battle of Shiloh was leveled at him by the press and by politicians. Iowa Senator James Harlan challenged the masculinity of those not agreeing with him when he proclaimed, "With such a record, those who continue General Grant in active command will in my opinion carry on their skirts the blood of thousands of their slaughtered countrymen."

But Grant's abject determination would prevail over numerous setbacks and enduring criticism in a career that would take him on to become the general-in-chief of all Union armies in 1864 and the commander-in-chief of the nation in 1869.

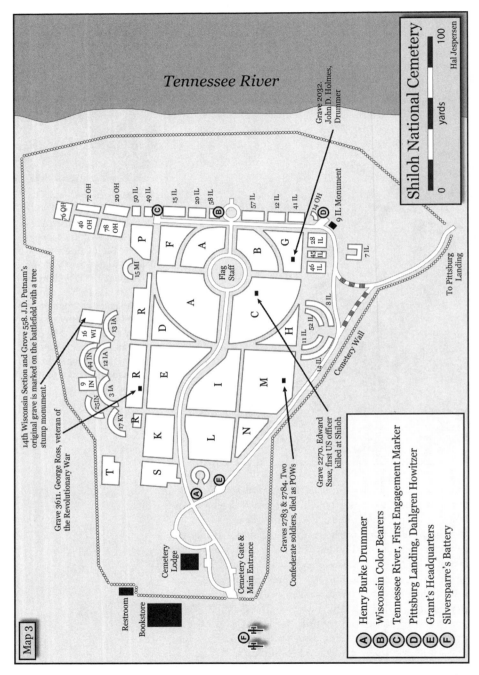

SHILOH NATIONAL CEMETERY—The tour of the Shiloh National Cemetery points out several interesting aspects of the layout and establishment of the cemetery, visits the important river port of Pittsburg Landing on the Tennessee River, and visits the site of U.S. Grant's headquarters on the night after the first day's battle.

At the National Cemetery

Across the parking lot from the visitor center is a large brick structure housing the park bookstore. Walk to the right of the bookstore to the large black with gold trim gateway at the entrance to the National Cemetery.

The National Cemetery is the final resting place for the vast majority of the Union soldiers who were killed at the battle of Shiloh, and a tour of the battlefield begins with a half-mile round-trip walk among their graves.

The beautiful, peaceful setting of the National Cemetery and the orderly alignment of the gravestones of today are in direct contradiction to the unsightly, chaotic, and brutal battlefield of 1862 that the cemetery serves to commemorate. Once the battle of Shiloh had ended, the ghastly battlefield was in Union hands. Its soldiers immediately undertook the many daunting tasks of dealing with the detritus of war, including the massive chore of burying the human remains of both sides.

The dead were originally buried throughout the battlefield near where they had fallen. After the war, this cemetery was established to properly honor those Union soldiers who made the ultimate sacrifice.

By regulation, the National Cemetery contains only the remains of United States military veterans. Even though former Confederate soldiers who survived the war would have a path to become United States citizens soon after the end of the Civil War, those who had fallen in opposition to the United States government would not be given the same consideration as the fallen Union soldiers. The Confederate

Just as the soldiers now lie in graves side by side in the cemetery, so Iowa soldier John T. Bell noted when examining the fresh battlefield that "[i]n places dead men lay so closely that a person could walk over two acres of ground and not step off the bodies." The daunting task of appropriately reburying the Union soldiers who died in the battle, as well as all those who died elsewhere in the Tennessee Valley—a five-state region—fell to Edmund B. Whitman. The Harvard graduate served as chief quartermaster during the Civil War. Whitman suggested that the hillside above Pittsburg Landing would be an ideal setting for such a solemn post. (cm)

Three Confederate soldiers who were prisoners of war and in Union hands when they died are buried in the National Cemetery. The graves of R. E. Cook from the 18th Alabama and Philip Prosser from the 13th Louisiana are marked with pointed stones, whereas the gravestones of Union soldiers are rounded on the top. F.A. Rasch of the Orleans Guard was the third Confederate buried in the cemetery, but he lies in an unknown grave. (gam)

Before reaching the rows upon rows of graves in the cemetery, visitors encounter the lone grave of what appears to be a drummer boy. The soldier buried in this grave is most likely named "Heinrich Budke" rather than "Henry Burke." (gam)

John Clem is one of the young soldiers whose life has greatly contributed to the mystique of the drummer boys. Clem was said to be just ten years old when he played his drum at Shiloh. Though Clem was a real drummer boy, he belonged to a unit that had not yet been recruited at the time the battle of Shiloh was fought, and it is doubtful whether he was actually in the fight. (loc)

soldiers still rest on the battlefield in multiple mass graves, five of which are identified on the battlefield today.

The primary mission of moving Union soldiers to the National Cemetery was completed by 1869. The burial details had interred 3,584 Civil War soldiers in the National Cemetery—apparently 1,874 of whom were killed or mortally wounded at Shiloh with the remainder transported here from sites of other battles or skirmishes in the Tennessee Valley. Most of the buried soldiers are unknown—only 620 of the dead from the battle of Shiloh rest in graves that are identified by name.

Walk straight down the walkway. Before reaching the rows upon rows of graves, stop at the lone headstone to the right of the walkway inscribed "Henry Burke— Drummer— 58th Ohio Infantry" in grave 3598 (stop 1A). The prominent placement of this interment by the designers of the cemetery was evidently meant to perpetuate the mistaken notion that it was common for very young drummer boys to be members of Civil War units. Though the soldier resting in the first grave encountered by most visitors to the National Cemetery appears to be that of a drummer boy named Henry Burke, he was likely not a drummer, likely not a young boy, and his name likely was not identified properly. No one named Henry Burke was in that regiment—a group of about 500 men identified by a number, state, and branch. The soldier buried in the grave is most likely Heinrich Budke, who died on April 28, 1862. Budke was member of the 58th Ohio regimental band and seems to have been in his 20s.

Continue down the brick walkway. Upon reaching the circular walk around the flagpole, go in either direction to reach the steps on the opposite side of the circle. The Tennessee River is at the bottom of the hill in front of you. It flows north, to your left as you observe the river. Walk down the steps and continue to a small circular walkway around a semicircle of six graves of Wisconsin soldiers (stop 1B).

Among the several special burial features included in the cemetery design, none is more impressive than that of the

Six color-bearers of the 16th Wisconsin—which fought in Spain Field and then in the Hornets' Nest on the first day of the battle—are buried in a semi-circle near the edge of the bluff overlooking the river. (gam)

Wisconsin Color Guard. The colors or flags were not only symbols of honor and pride for soldiers' units, but in the deafening noise of battle, flags were a visual indication of where units were supposed to be on the field of battle. It was important that the colors never fall, so the members of the unit could see the location of the center of the regimental battle line. Shooting down the opposing color-bearer, on the other hand, could cause confusion in the ranks of the enemy. These six men of the 16th Wisconsin Infantry all understood the importance of making sure their flags were held aloft and died performing that critical mission.

While facing the graves of the Wisconsin color bearers, turn left and follow the brick walkway to its end. There find a tablet with a blue border and red lettering, titled "First Engagement on Shiloh Battlefield" (stop 1C).

Read the "First Engagement on Shiloh Battlefield" for more information about the March 1, 1862, fight that occurred here. Then walk back past the graves of the Wisconsin Color Bearers, continuing straight ahead to a bronze howitzer with "DAHLGREN" engraved across the top, mounted on a white concrete base (stop 1D).

Looking in the direction the howitzer is pointing, the circular drive visible to your right front at the bottom of the hill is Pittsburg Landing. Logistics are essential to an army. Wherever the Union army happened to set up camp along the Tennessee River, it required a suitable port where supply boats could dock and unload the food, fodder, and other material needed by the men and animals comprising this massive army. Pittsburg Landing met that need.

As you continue walking along the brick walkway, keep to the right where the steps lead down to Pittsburg Landing. Stop at the three upright cannon marking Grant's Headquarters (stop 1E). The cannon pyramid stands at the site of the tree under which Grant spent the night of April 6-7.

The monument to the 9th Illinois is the only regimental monument in the National Cemetery and, unlike virtually all other regimental monuments in the park, it does not mark a battle position. The monument honors the regiment that probably has more men buried in this cemetery than any other. It suffered the heaviest loss of any Union unit at Shiloh—366 killed and wounded out of 578 men present for duty. (In the movie shown in the visitor center, this is the unit that young Cockerill found himself attached to after he became separated from his father's regiment.) (gam)

Continue down the walkway, turn left at the next intersection, and exit the cemetery. Walk across the concrete sidewalk to your left-front to the two cannon with a monument between them, marking the position of Silversparre's Battery H, 1st Illinois Artillery (stop 1F). Notice that the monument indicates that "the guns were brought by hand to this position" and that the unit was "unassigned."

Silversparre's Battery H, 1st Illinois Artillery, is a first-rate example of many of the issues faced by green units joining an army still in the process of being organized.

The artillery in both armies were set up into units called batteries, typically consisting of four or six cannon, their gun crews, and horses to pull the cannon and the ammunition caissons. Once Silversparre's Battery disembarked at Pittsburg Landing on the day before the battle, it was unable to go anywhere else because it still lacked one of the essential components of a battery: horses. The gunners had no option other than to manhandle their four cannon up the slope and into a position just above the landing (your current location), where it was engaged during the afternoon of the first day of the battle.

The Union Army of the Tennessee, numbering some 48,000 men, grouped all of its units into six divisions of about 7,000 men each. Most of the divisions were made up of three brigades numbering about 2,000 men each. The divisions also contained an average of three artillery batteries and about 200 cavalrymen.

Unable to sleep due to an injured ankle and the driving rain, Gen. Ulysses S. Grant kept vigil the night of April 6-7 under a tree that came down during a cyclone in 1909. Today, a pyramid of cannon marks Grant's headquarters. (gam)(gam)

As Grant's army was still being forged, new units arrived and were being outfitted daily. Its configuration was incomplete on the eve of the battle and when the opening shots were fired several units that had arrived were yet to be assigned to a particular division.

Regiments and batteries led by men with solid military experience were the exception rather than the rule. Throughout both armies, colonels, lieutenant colonels, and majors leading the regiments or captains commanding batteries were selected because they were leaders in their communities, or were highly educated, or held responsible positions. These people were accustomed to making important decisions in civilian life or presumably possessed the intellect to enable them to learn how to become leaders of soldiers. Politicians, lawyers, prominent businessmen with no or very limited military experience filled the ranks of the officers leading the regiments and batteries in the armies at Shiloh—and were often the leaders in several brigades and divisions as well.

Battery H, 1st Illinois Artillery, fared better than most units in regard to its leadership. The battery was commanded by Capt. Axel Silversparre (or Silfversparre), a former lieutenant in the Swedish army who had just immigrated to the United States in 1861. The majority of his men were also Swedish Americans, who did not like the strict discipline exacted by their experienced captain.

As with many of the units on the Shiloh battlefield, Silversparre's Battery not only had no battle experience, but they had virtually no training. Grant's chief of staff, Col. Joseph D. Webster, found time to run Silversparre's green gun crews through the drill of firing a cannon, shooting it in the direction of the Confederate army. They had the unique experience of firing at actual Confederate soldiers—not imaginary targets—as they practiced and honed their skills while an actual battle raged all around them.

Virtually all of the artillery pieces on the battlefield—like these from Silversparre's Battery—are actual Civil War cannon. The carriages are reproductions: pieces of the carriage that would have been made of wood are painted a shade of green, while pieces that would have been iron are painted black. The men comprising batteries and companies (ten companies make up a regiment) were raised in the same communities, so many of those serving side by side were relatives, neighbors and friends. (gam)

➤ TO STOP 2

Exit the parking lot and turn right. Drive 0.1 mile and park at the pull-off on the right. The tall Iowa monument will be on your right.

Carefully walk across to the left side of road to the concrete orientation station (stop 2A). As you face the exhibits, you are looking south.

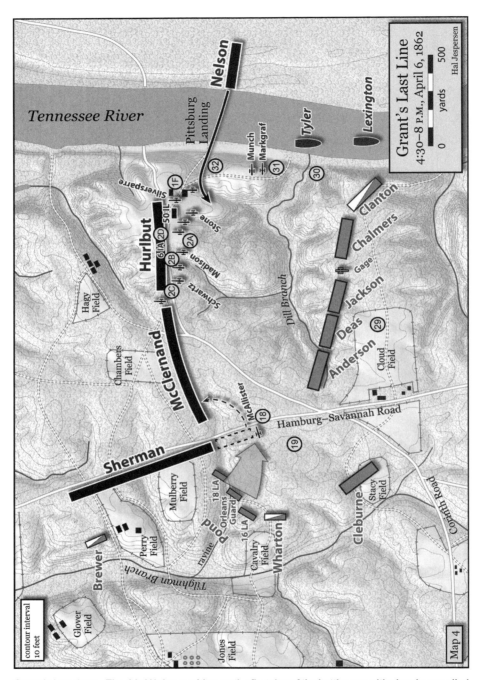

GRANT'S LAST LINE—The third Union position on the first day of the battle was critical and was called Grant's Last Line because there was no more space and no more defensible terrain to protect the Union supply and transportation base at Pittsburg Landing. Bolstered with cannon positioned behind steep ravines and aided by gunboats, the Union stronghold withstood Confederate attacks launched about 6:00 p.m.

Dill Branch is in front and the road behind is the historic Corinth Road. The row of cannon and monuments in this area mark part of Grant's Last Line.

At Grant's Last Line

"Grant's Last Line" is an intriguing name, considering it represents a position held in the middle of a two-day fight during which Grant's army actually would hold many subsequent positions before the battle concluded. The position is, however, the last possible piece of ground that the Union army could defend before it would be compelled to abandon its line of supplies and line of evacuation at Pittsburg Landing. Neither distance to the landing nor the terrain would permit the Union army to hold another defensible position without giving up the critical landing.

The Union army occupied three primary positions during the first day of the battle. The first line was about three miles from Pittsburg Landing in the outlying Union camps where the morning fighting lasted from about 7:00 to 11:00. The second position was about one-and-one-half miles from Pittsburg Landing, centered on what has come to be known as the "Sunken Road." The timing of this fight was from approximately 10:00 a.m. to 6:00 p.m.

This area now named "Grant's Last Line" was the third position held by the Union army. The fight for this position occurred over an afternoon timespan from roughly 4:00 to 8:00. Grant's third line made excellent use of the terrain features to form a nearly impregnable defensive position. The line anchored its left flank on the banks of the Tennessee less than one-quarter mile south of Pittsburg Landing. From the landing, Grant's final defensive stand ran west for almost a mile (including your current location), overlooking the intimidating valley of Dill Branch. At the time of the war, much of Dill Branch was void of the woods found there today, and the soldiers occupying the line had the ability to observe any attacking forces.

A nearly 90-degree bend marked the center of Grant's crucial defense. The right wing of the line extended north from the angle and was posted along the Hamburg-

Pyramids of cannonballs, like the one in the middle of the photograph, mark Union headquarters in the camps. The three obelisk monuments behind the siege artillery are Indiana unit markers. The states of Illinois and Iowa also mark the battle positions of its regiments with identical monuments. Ohio marks the positions of its units, as well; however, each monument is unique. Pennsylvania and Minnesota each erected a unit monument to the solitary unit from their state that fought at Shiloh. Wisconsin, Alabama, Tennessee, and Louisiana also each placed one regimental marker on the field. (gam)

Savannah Road behind the formidable valley of Tilghman Branch. The right flank was solidly anchored on the swollen Owl Creek.

Besides the natural strength of the position, the Union forces further secured the line with the most powerful and most daunting weapons in the army: siege guns. Walk to your right across the historic roadbed of the Corinth Road, and stop at the next set of cannon—the largest cannon in the vicinity—and the Illinois monument that reads "Siege Guns" on the front (stop 2B). These siege guns are the same type as those that Madison's Illinois Battery fired from this position.

The artillery amassed at Grant's Last Line, with the steep banks, high water and open ground of Dill Branch in front, presented both a firepower and a terrain that the Confederates—exhausted, disorganized and low on ammunition—could not overcome. (bl)

The final Confederate attack of the first day of the battle was made against this position, Grant's Last Line, at about 6:00 p.m. Ironically, the attack was launched against the strongest portion of that line—a point on the left wing where the Union army had massed an impressive array of artillery.

That intimidating collection of cannon began to take shape about 2:30 p.m. when Grant turned to his chief of staff, Col. Joseph D. Webster. The Dartmouth graduate and engineer was tasked with massing artillery around which the withdrawing army could rally and which might blast away any Confederate attackers.

Webster began by positioning batteries that had not been good candidates for service elsewhere on the battlefield. Most prominent were the impressive looking siege artillery pieces of Madison's Battery B, 2nd Illinois Light Artillery. Siege or heavy artillery batteries were designed to be slowly maneuvered into semi-permanent positions, suitable for long-term siege operations as they were too heavy and cumbersome to haul easily around on a fluid battlefield. Field or light artillery batteries, conversely, were light enough to frequently change positions and be moved around on an active battlefield.

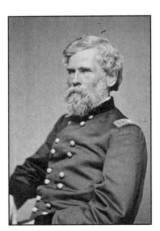

Joseph D. Webster, a 50-year-old native of New Hampshire, held a commission with the army topographical engineers for sixteen years. His eye for terrain contributed to the strength of Grant's Last Line. (loc)

The Union army anticipated that the Confederates would dig fortifications around Corinth and await the Union army to initiate the spring 1862 campaign. Accordingly, Union forces were prepared for long, drawn-out siege operations at the rail hub, and brought along the huge siege artillery pieces for that anticipated purpose. But with the change in plans brought about by the sudden Confederate attack at Shiloh, these huge guns were put in service for a purpose different from that for which they were designed. The siege guns were called upon to buttress Grant's last chance defense. Soon other guns from elsewhere on the battlefield were added to the unassigned batteries that had been the origin of Grant's Last Line.

Continue walking farther down the line of cannon, past the tablet and cannon marking Richardson's Battery, to the tablet and guns for Schwartz's Battery E, 2nd Illinois Light Artillery (stop 2C). Be very careful to only look at and not walk upon the fragile remains of the earthworks in front of these cannon.

Cannon are usually identified either by the diameter of the bore in inches, or by the weight of the solid shot fired by the cannon. The short-barreled gun is an eight-inch siege howitzer (the bore diameter). The long-barreled cannon are 24-pounder siege guns (the weight of the solid shot). (gam)

Some of the units that had already fought for long hours on other portions of the battlefield were called upon to augment the final position of the day, going into action yet again. All in all, Webster amassed some fifty artillery pieces as the foundation for this final line—an amount of firepower perhaps only exceeded on American soil by the Confederates just a few hours earlier in the day to pound the second Union position.

Schwartz's Illinois Battery was one of several artillery units that had been previously engaged in the battle before contributing to Grant's Last Line. Its commander, Lt. George L. Nispel, reported that his artillery occupied its sixth position of the day when ordered to "take a position on the right of the siege guns and support them."

About 6:00 p.m., the Confederates made their final attack for the day, and Nispel's men sprung to action once again. He wrote, "The enemy advancing, a heavy fire was opened on him, the most terrific I ever heard. Every one seemed to be imbued with the idea that as this was our last stand, so should it be the most desperate."

When the Union soldiers repulsed the attack, they did not know that it would in fact conclude the day's fighting. "Thinking the enemy during the darkness of the night might make an attempt to charge and capture our guns," Nispel disclosed, "I threw up a little breastwork, and self and men laid there all night." The term "breastwork" conveys the height of the dirt fortifications—infantrymen in particular, would pile soil up to the height of their breast or chest.

While earthworks eventually became prominent features, they were generally not constructed as part of battlefield defensive positions during the phase of the war in which the battle of Shiloh was fought. Schwartz's Battery position is one of the very few places at Shiloh where the soldiers built works. (gam)

Cross the Corinth Road and walk back toward the tall Iowa monument. Along the way note the location of the blue tablet acknowledging the 40th Illinois and the 6th Iowa. Continue to the Iowa monument (stop 2D).

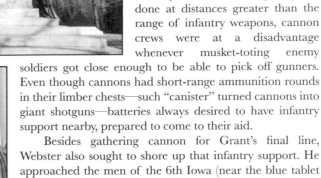

Stand at the corner at the front of the monument, on the side with the woman representing "Fame" climbing the steps to inscribe the deeds of the eleven regiments from the state that fought at Shiloh.

With your back to the Iowa monument, look to your left front across the Corinth Road and across a slight ravine. Notice the row of four cannon on the next knoll, close to the current wood line. This is the position of Stone's Missouri Battery. About 15 yards to the rear of Stone's position, notice a blue tablet; it marks the position of the 50th Illinois.

Although artillery units typically held an advantage over opposing infantry whenever the fighting was done at distances greater than the range of infantry weapons, cannon crews were at a disadvantage whenever musket-toting enemy soldiers got close enough to be able to pick off gunners. Even though cannons had short-range ammunition rounds in their limber chests—such "canister" turned cannons into giant shotguns—batteries always desired to have infantry support nearby, prepared to come to their aid.

Besides gathering cannon for Grant's final line, Webster also sought to shore up that infantry support. He approached the men of the 6th Iowa (near the blue tablet to your right) to direct them to be prepared in case the anticipated fight became hand to hand: "I pledge you my men at the guns will do their duty," Webster swore, "and if the Rebels come on, I want you to meet them with the cold steel." By calling upon them to use "cold steel," Webster was imploring them to use their bayonets if necessary.

Standing 75 feet high, the Iowa monument is the tallest monument in the park. Climbing the steps on the east side of the monument is a woman representing "Fame," inscribing the deeds of the eleven regiments from the state that fought at Shiloh. (gam)(gam)

Stone's Battery K, 1st Missouri Artillery, was able to foster its infantry support from the 50th Illinois (to your left front). Stone's men had just been driven from the second Union position on a ridge behind the Sunken Road by a massive collection of Confederate artillery. Now the battery was part of a Union artillery stronghold that was almost as powerful as one they had faced only moments earlier.

The anticipated Confederate attack came early in the evening of April 6 when about 4,000 infantrymen advanced across the broad Dill Branch, tackling its steep banks and its high water. Confederate artillery opened as well. Grant was in the thick of the bombardment, experiencing a close call. At a point just to the left of the siege guns, a messenger delivered a dispatch to Grant. The departing courier, only a few yards distant, was decapitated by a Confederate artillery projectile.

Some Confederates made it to the edge of the ravine about one-quarter mile from Grant's line. Stone's Battery and the portion of the 50th Illinois to their left opened fire, along with other units of this last line. A member of the 50th Illinois succinctly described the Confederate attack: "As soon as they reached the top of the hill in front, the batteries opened upon them, and such cannonading I never heard before. It completely checked the rebels."

Another account from a soldier in the 50th Illinois made the following observation about the final stages of the attack:

> It was a happy moment to me when they gave way and fell back. From our position we could see General Grant sitting on his horse near the top of the hill to our left, and a part of the time Surgeon Kendal with him. . . . [D]uring the rebel charge, when it looked as though they might drive us into the river, [Kendal] said, 'General, things are going decidedly against us to-day,' which drew forth one of Grant's characteristic replies, 'Not at all, sir. We are whipping them there now.' The result proved his remark true but I venture the assertion there was not another man in the army who would have made it at that particular time.

As the Union artillery fire tapered off following the repulse of the Confederate attack, Lt. Horace Fisher, temporarily serving on Grant's staff, reported to the general: "I rode forward, saluted, and waited for his order. He paid no attention. His eyes were fixed to the front. Again I heard him mutter something without turning. Then I saw he was talking to himself, 'Not beaten yet by a damn sight.'"

Grant's Last Line had held, and with reinforcements arriving that night, the Union army would take its turn launching an offensive of its own on the second day of the battle.

➤ **TO STOP 3**

Return to your car. Drive 0.25 mile and turn left. Drive another 0.9 mile to the pull-off on the right for the Confederate monument. Carefully cross the road and walk up to the monument. In the middle of the monument, beneath the three central figures, is the bust of Gen. A. S. Johnston.

The Confederates Stir

CHAPTER TWO

April 3-6, 1862

On the Confederate memorial, an infantryman represents defiance, grasping the battle flag so it does not fall to the ground, while an artilleryman calmly gazes forward. Elsewhere on the monument, a cavalryman displays frustration because the terrain at Shiloh hampers the ability of the mounted branch to contribute to the battle, while an officer looks submissive—he must obey what he feels is an unfortunate order to halt the attack on the first day of battle before the Confederates had achieved a complete victory. (cm)

Fifty-nine-year-old Kentucky-born and Texas-adopted Albert Sidney Johnston was regarded as one of the most capable soldiers throughout the South. To Johnston—the second-highest ranking general in the Confederacy—fell responsibility for defending all key points across a huge department from the Appalachian Mountains to present-day Oklahoma.

However, under Johnston's watch, Fort Henry fell, and Fort Donelson surrendered, giving up its large garrison and severely tarnishing Johnston's previously bright reputation. After he abandoned most of western and central Tennessee, all but one member of the Tennessee congressional delegation called for Johnston's removal "because he is no general." Confederate President Jefferson Davis stood by his long-time friend: "If [Johnston] is not a general, we had better give up the war," proclaimed Davis, "for we have no general."

While Davis did not waiver in his confidence in Johnston, he did change his mind about one important policy. Johnston would no longer be hampered with the expectation that he distribute his troops to defend concurrently multiple points in his department. He was permitted to mass troops to form a sizeable army. His forces soon concentrated near the railroad junction of Corinth, Mississippi.

On April 3, 1862, before all of the troops intended to make up the new Army of the Mississippi had arrived, it became obvious that the Confederates could wait no longer. Word came that Buell's army was nearing its juncture with Grant's army. It was more important to strike Grant before Buell's arrival than to await more Southern reinforcements.

Realizing that the spring rains had swollen the streams around Grant's forces, Johnston planned to strike hard and then sweep his army behind the Union camps, cutting them

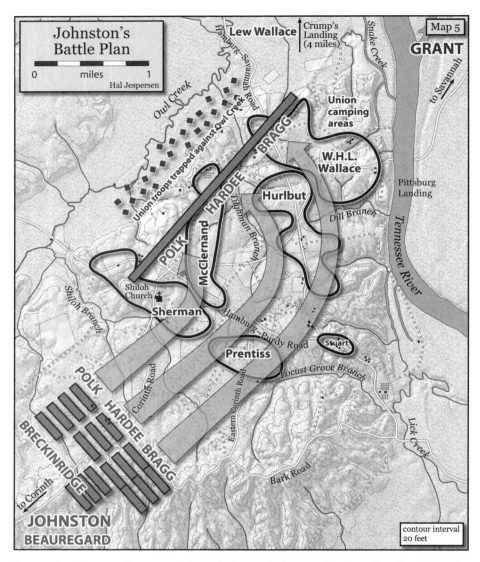

Johnston's Battle Plan
Map 5

0   miles   1
Hal Jespersen

GRANT

Lew Wallace

Crump's Landing (4 miles)

Union camping areas

W.H.L. Wallace

Pittsburg Landing

Hurlbut

Union troops trapped against Owl Creek

BRAGG

HARDEE

POLK

McClernand

Dill Branch

Tennessee River

Tilghman Branch

Shiloh Church

Sherman

Hamburg-Purdy Road

Stuart

Prentiss

Locust Grove Branch

POLK   HARDEE   BRAGG

BRECKINRIDGE

Corinth Road

Eastern Corinth Road

to Corinth

Bark Road

Lick Creek

JOHNSTON
BEAUREGARD

contour interval 20 feet

JOHNSTON'S BATTLE PLAN— Johnston relayed his planned battle formation to Jefferson Davis on April 3: "Polk, left; Hardee, center; Bragg, right wing; Breckinridge, reserve." Johnston intended for the corps to be side by side, giving each corps commander a distinct, compact sector for greater command and control, with initial reserves from their own corps readily on call.

off from their supply base at Pittsburg Landing. Then by trapping the Union forces against the flooded Owl Creek to the north, Confederates would destroy Grant's army—in similar fashion to the way Grant had trapped and destroyed the Confederates at Fort Donelson.

The march to Shiloh was slow, and troops poised to attack were forced to wait until the rest of the army came up. On the evening of April 5, the night before the battle, some of the Confederate high command thought that the Union army had certainly been alerted to the presence of the Confederate army and felt the element of surprise had been lost.

"Now they will be entrenched to the eyes," predicted

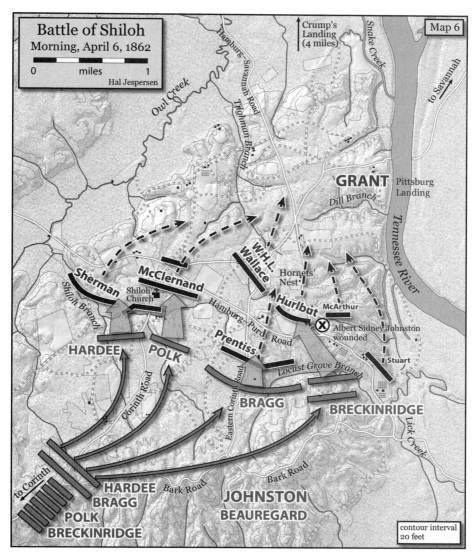

Battle of Shiloh
Morning, April 6, 1862

0   miles   1
Hal Jespersen

Crump's Landing (4 miles)

Map 6

GRANT   Pittsburg Landing

Dill Branch

W.H.L. Wallace

Hornets' Nest

McClernand

Shiloh Church

Sherman

Hurlbut

McArthur

(X) Albert Sidney Johnston wounded

HARDEE   POLK

Prentiss

Stuart

Hamburg-Purdy Road

Locust Grove Branch

BRAGG

BRECKINRIDGE

Corinth Road

Eastern Corinth Road

to Corinth

HARDEE   Bark Road
BRAGG
POLK
BRECKINRIDGE

Bark Road

JOHNSTON
BEAUREGARD

Lick Creek

contour interval 20 feet

Owl Creek

Shiloh Branch

Hamburg-Savannah Road

Tilghman Branch

Snake Creek

to Savannah

Tennessee River

Johnston's second in command, Gen. Pierre G. T. Beauregard. Some of the other generals present were of like mind. After enduring a difficult march, delaying the planned start of the battle, and finally getting the entire army into position, Johnston's highest-ranking subordinates advised turning around and going back to Corinth.

The situation was similar to the one Grant would encounter the following evening when so many Union officers thought that retreat was their best course of action. Facing similar opposition both generals showed their resolve.

"We shall attack them at daylight tomorrow," Johnston announced to his discouraged generals. The magnanimous Johnston had involved his subordinates in the planning

BATTLE OF SHILOH—Beauregard, entrusted with executing Johnston's plan, either did not understand or ignored Johnston's desired battle formation. The Confederate corps were stacked up one behind the other rather than side by side. Corps commanders found it impossible to command and control their troops, with portions of their corps spread out across the entire battlefront.

Confederate Council of War, April 5, 1862: Left to right, second in command P.G.T, Beauregard, 1st Corps commander Leonidas Polk (seated), Reserve Corps commander John C. Breckenridge, army commander A. S. Johnston, 2nd Corps commander Braxton Bragg, and engineer Maj. Jeremy. F. Gilmer. Despite opposition from some at the council of war, Johnston was adamant that the Confederates should attack because the Union army was still confined within the small space between Lick and Owl Creeks, where he felt his Confederates could pin the enemy against the Owl Creek swamps. (loc)

Unlike Johnston, P. G. T. Beauregard had achieved successes thus far in the Civil War. He had directed the bombardment and surrender of Fort Sumter to start the war and had been the field general in the victory at the battle of First Manassas. (na)

of the campaign and had welcomed their input, but the decisive moment had arrived, and time for further discussion had passed.

"I would fight them if they were a million," a determined Johnston told a member of his staff as he walked away from the gathering. "They can present no greater front between these two creeks than we can," Johnston explained, "and the more men they crowd in there, the worse we can make it for them."

On the morning of April 6, Beauregard renewed his cynicism, but the sounds of gunfire interrupted the discussion. "The battle has opened, gentlemen," the army commander remarked, "It is too late to change our dispositions." Johnston mounted his thoroughbred, Fire-Eater, and announced to his staff, "Tonight, we will water our horses in the Tennessee River."

Johnston also revealed, apparently for the first time, that his place during the battle would be at the front. Beauregard would stay in the rear, sending troops where needed most.

It has often been noted that Johnston seemingly abdicated command of the army to his second in command. Perhaps Johnston felt that recent surgery and illness prevented Beauregard from taking on a more vigorous role. Perhaps Johnston felt that the pessimism of the high command now required his leadership and inspiration at the front. For whatever reason, Johnston played an active role, spending the vast majority of his time on the Confederate right making important decisions and adjustments to carry out the plan of turning the Union left and shoving them into the swollen Owl Creek. While at the front, directing the fighting against the Union second position, Johnston was mortally wounded about 2:30 p.m.

Some three hours later, the Confederates neared Pittsburg Landing and Grant's final defensive position. Despite much success earlier that day, the Confederates now were tired, disorganized, low on or out of ammunition, and running out of daylight. Though the first attack on Grant's line failed, Gen. Jones M. Withers was preparing to attack again when he noticed the troops to his left were pulling back. Upon investigating the reason for this seemingly disgraceful behavior, Withers discovered that the troops had withdrawn under orders to disengage—orders from Beauregard, now directing the army. Beauregard believed they would finish off the Union army the next day.

Unfortunately for Beauregard, the Union army was heavily reinforced throughout the night and retook its camps on the second day of the battle.

Albert Sidney Johnston was named the highest-ranking field officer in all of Confederate service. Although his second in command, Beauregard, had run afoul of President Davis and thought service under Johnston was some type of punishment, the army commander took his disgruntled subordinate into his confidence and entrusted him with important responsibilities. (bl)

At the Confederate Monument

Shiloh's Confederate monument offers one interpretation of the reason the Confederates lost the battle of Shiloh. The monument tells the story of the battle from the point of view that the decision to end the fighting after just one attack against Grant's third line was a mistake. Whether or not another attack at this place and time *should* have been made has always been a controversial aspect of the battle.

The three women at the center of the statue are collectively known as "Defeated Victory." The central figure represents the Confederacy, flanked by two figures who represent "Death" and "Night." As Death and Night closed in on the Confederacy, they led to defeat. The sculptor carved the bust of Albert Sidney Johnston into the monument, front and center, just beneath the trio of statutes.

The monument not only depicts an interpretation of why the Confederates lost the battle of Shiloh, but gives a Southern explanation for why they lost the war, as well. The "Lost Cause" explanation of the Civil War offered the South a way to look upon defeat with honor. Key principles of the Lost Cause include the conviction that leaders with high integrity either fell in battle or were let down by subordinates, and that the Confederates were defeated by overwhelming numbers and resources.

⟶ TO STOP 4

Continue driving down the Corinth Road for 0.8 mile. (Skip the pull-offs for Duncan Field and Ruggles's Battery—we will visit those points later when we can cover the action there in a more chronological manner.) Veer left at the fork in the road and continue 0.1 mile. Turn right onto the Hamburg-Purdy Road and drive another 0.1 mile. Turn left back onto the Corinth Road and drive 0.3 mile to a pull-off on the right. The parking lot for Shiloh Methodist Church will be on your left. Walk to the orientation station ahead of the pull-off (stop 4A).

The Confederate monument, erected by the United Daughters of the Confederacy in 1917, is known for both its splendor and its symbolism. The UDC selected a design by sculptor Frederick C. Hibbard that tells one version of why the Confederates lost the battle of Shiloh. (gam)

Eleven Confederates on the right half of the monument eagerly head into battle. (gam)

A woman representing the Confederacy (center) surrenders the laurel of victory to the woman signifying Death (left), which has taken her army commander at a critical moment of the battle. The cloaked woman, Night (right), also deprived the Confederacy of victory, the monument contends, because reinforcements filled the Union ranks throughout the night. (gam)

Johnston is not only central to the physical design of the monument, but also to the message it conveys. Part of the Lost Cause interpretation of the battle of Shiloh is that, had Johnston not been shot, he would have attacked Grant's Last Line and successfully driven it back, taking Pittsburg Landing and delivering a Confederate victory. This explanation not only professes to know what Johnston would have done, but how well he would have fared in pursuing that supposed course of action. (gam)

Confederates on the left of the monument, reduced from eleven to ten due to casualties, are dejected because they have lost a battle that they feel they had nearly won. (gam)

The Battle Opens at Shiloh Church

CHAPTER THREE

April 6, 1862—early to mid-morning

Brigadier General William T. Sherman had been given a second chance. Accused of being insane earlier in the war, he had lost a prime assignment. Back in a command position at Shiloh, Sherman was resolved to be a loyal subordinate to the general who had allowed him another opportunity.

A 42-year-old West Point graduate, Sherman had once been in charge of the Department of the Cumberland—basically the same post Don Carlos Buell now held. But Sherman saw grave danger from Confederates in Kentucky and called for what was deemed to be an unrealistic army of 200,000 Union soldiers. The weight of responsibility was too much for Sherman, who may have suffered a nervous breakdown, and he was relieved of command.

Sherman was then assigned to a training camp in St. Louis, which was also the headquarters of the Department of the Missouri, commanded by Maj. Gen. Henry Halleck. Halleck included Sherman in strategic discussions and became impressed with his abilities. Halleck felt that Sherman was right for a command that subsequently became a new division under Grant.

Sherman wisely posted his troops to guard the key roads leading into the camp at Shiloh. He straddled the important road to Corinth on a ridge where the road passed by the simple, log Shiloh Meeting House (your location). Significantly, the Union position overlooked a pair of streams—Shiloh Branch and its East Branch (ahead of you)—which because of the heavy spring rains created a substantial swampy barrier to any attacking Confederates.

Though guarding the roads and patrolling the area just beyond the Union camps would be standard practice for the security for the army, it was widely believed that the Confederates would not be a threat and would not

A structure similar to this reconstruction was built in 1853 at the site of the modern church and witnessed the battle. Ironically, the word "Shiloh" in Hebrew means "place of peace." (cm)

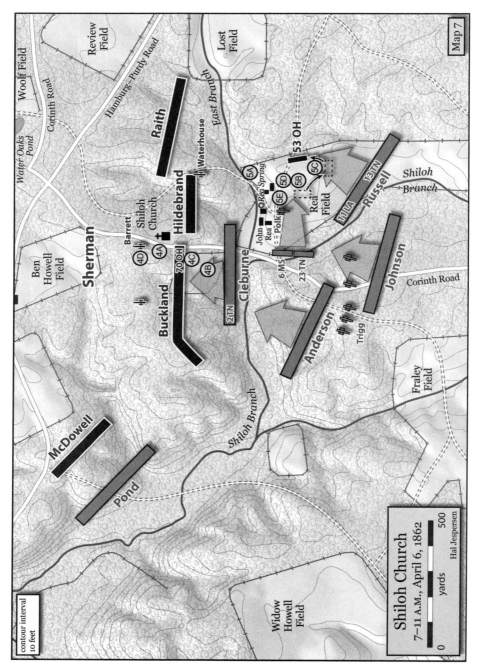

Shiloh Church
7–11 a.m., April 6, 1862

Hal Jespersen

0   yards   500

contour interval
10 feet

Map 7

Shiloh Church—Though Union Gen. William T. Sherman refused to accept notice from his subordinates of a nearby Confederate buildup, his troops withstood repeated Confederate attacks hampered by crossing rain swollen streams in front of the Union position and lack of coordination among Confederate units.

come anywhere near Shiloh Meeting House, often now called "Shiloh Church." It was expected that instead the Confederates would fortify Corinth and put the onus upon the Union army to drive them out.

The Union army was more than willing to oblige by launching a campaign against Corinth, but it would make the effort only after the armies of Grant and Buell merged and Halleck took command of the combined forces. In the meantime, Halleck's orders were that Grant's army was to avoid a general engagement with the Confederates. Sherman, who owed his new assignment to the confidence that Halleck had placed in him, was determined to elude battle with the enemy, even when it appeared to many of those around him that Confederates were nearby in force.

Though Sherman received many reports of small numbers of Confederates spotted on the outskirts of his camps, he did not consider that the combined reports might suggest that a substantial number of Confederate troops were but a short distance away. The man, who as a department commander in Kentucky had overreacted on intelligence of Confederate strengths, now seemingly overcompensated as a division commander by underreacting to reports of a Confederate build-up on the fringes of his encampment.

As the only West Point-trained division commander in Grant's army, Sherman's advice and observations were highly esteemed. On the day before the battle began, Sherman informed Grant, "I do not apprehend anything like an attack on our position." Based upon that assessment, Grant sent a similar message to Halleck: "I have scarcely the faintest idea of an attack (general one) being made upon us." The messages would prove to be exceedingly embarrassing for each general. Fortunately for Sherman, his subordinates were not of like mind. They continued to send out patrols, strengthen pickets, and pass along reports detailing sightings of Confederates—despite ridicule these subordinates received from Sherman.

Although Sherman was confident that the Confederates on the peripheries of his camp were just small reconnoitering parties, in fact, the entire Confederate army was poised to assault, and his division would be one of their first targets. Brigadier General Patrick R. Cleburne led the Confederate brigade that attacked at the church. After Cleburne observed the white tents of Sherman's camp, he turned to Capt. John T. Trigg, commanding an Arkansas battery attached to his brigade, and ordered, "wake him up with a few shells." At 7:10 on the morning of April 6, the Confederates fired the first artillery shot of the battle from a ridge on the south side of Shiloh Branch, and soon afterwards the first wave of infantry assaulted Sherman's camp.

As the Union artillery responded, it became obvious

For a man who had evidently suffered a nervous breakdown months earlier when commanding a department, Sherman was remarkably calm and composed during the chaos of battle. He sent an aide to the army commander to explain the situation at Shiloh Church from his perspective: "Tell Grant if he has any men to spare I can use them; if not I will do the best I can. We are holding them pretty well just now— pretty well—but it's hot as hell." (loc)

that Trigg's guns were being hit from several directions and soon had to abandon Cleburne's infantry. That was just the start of the problems Cleburne faced attacking the ridge of the church. Though the corps of Maj. Gen. William J. Hardee—one of four corps comprising the Confederate army—had all stepped off together, a gap had developed between Cleburne and the troops on his right. So, Cleburne's isolated brigade initiated the assault on Sherman's camps on its own.

Then Cleburne's detached brigade encountered the thickly wooded and swampy Shiloh Branch and East Branch terrain extending across in front of Sherman's troops. "An almost impassable morass,"

While attacking the Union stronghold at Shiloh Church, Lt. Col. Thomas H. Peeples of the 24th Tennessee had his horse shot from under him and despite multiple holes in his uniform from piercing bullets, he amazingly made it through the battle without a wound. He later hugged a friend and wept, sharing that he could not help but feel that "Providence protected him" in the midst of such a hail of gunfire. (gam)

is how Cleburne described it, adding, "My own horse bogged down in it and threw me, and it was with great difficulty I got out." Cleburne's brigade split as it passed on either side of the swamp, so the brigade did not even fight together. The two regiments in his right wing initially fought in Rea Field to the east, while the four regiments of his left wing took on a Union brigade commanded by Ohio lawyer and politician Col. Ralph P. Buckland, positioned west of Shiloh Church.

Cleburne's brigade was the extreme left end of the entire Confederate line, and the 2nd Tennessee was the extreme left of Cleburne's command. After the Tennesseans struggled through the swollen streams of the Shiloh and East branches, they discovered that Buckland's line easily overlapped Cleburne's line, and the 2nd Tennessee was at risk of being struck in both its front and on its left flank.

Moving up to the front in the very footsteps of Cleburne, and splashing through the same muddy quagmire, was Brig. Gen. Patton Anderson's brigade of Maj. Gen. Braxton Bragg's corps in the second wave. However, even the reinforced Confederates could not drive Sherman from his camps by attacking Buckland's front.

*   *   *

Young John Cockerill observed the first Confederate attack against his father's regiment—the 70th Ohio in Buckland's command: "The sun was just rising in their front, and the glittering of their arms and equipments made a gorgeous spectacle."

Of some 385 men in the 2nd Tennessee to fight at Shiloh, 235 men were casualties—killed, wounded, captured, or missing—an astounding 65% loss. Many of them fell on the slopes of Shiloh Branch near where their monument stands. (cm)

"They poured out their deadly fire," John remembered, "and, half obscured by their smoke, they advanced as they fired."

Farther up the hill and to the left of the 70th Ohio, Barrett's Battery joined in the fray, and after firing just one round, young Cockerill noted that it "drew the fire of a Confederate battery." Positioned to the rear of any cannon was an ammunition chest on wheels, known as a "limber," and even farther back would have been three ammunition chests making up a separate wheeled vehicle, the caisson. "This duel had not lasted more than ten minutes when a Confederate shell struck a caisson in our battery," Cockerill observed, "and an explosion took place." Even when cannon firing at the enemy artillery happened to overshoot and miss their mark, damage could still be done by taking out the ammunition supply, as the Confederates did to Barrett's Battery.

After withdrawing and reforming his 2nd Tennessee regiment, Col. William B. Bate reported, "I moved the regiment to the right and then to the front, with the view of taking a battery which was then playing upon us." That battery was Barrett's artillery. Bate crept ahead of his troops for a closer examination as he tried to figure out how to best knock out the battery.

Sergeant Robert Smith later wrote that his commander "came out in front of what was left of our regiment and said, 'My brave boys, the enemy must be driven back. I am going to charge them again!! How many of you will follow me?' Without giving a command, he immediately took his position at the head of the regiment and waved his sword. As quick as

a thought every man had his bayonet on the charge and started, double quick up the hill. . . . Onward we pushed through that storm of bullets. . . . Here . . . our brave Col. fell, badly wounded." Colonel Bate was shot in the leg. His men caught him as he slid from his horse.

Even repeated, determined Confederate frontal attacks could not dislodge Sherman's men from the meeting house line. Sherman's men held their position for two hours before their line collapsed. What

Sherman reasoned why his green troops were able to hold out for some three hours against the Confederate onslaughts: "Our men were so posted as to have a good fire at him as he crossed the valley and ascended the rising ground on our side." The 70th Ohio's monument today marks some of that ground. (gam)

forced Sherman's men back from this ridge was a gap in the Union position to the east. Some 500 yards of ground with nary a Union soldier in it loomed large between Sherman's battle line and another hasty assemblage of troops from the neighboring division of Brig. Gen. Benjamin Prentiss.

Confederates exploited that gap, striking the flank and rear of Sherman's line east of the Corinth Road around the log church and beyond, driving them back. Union reserves came to Sherman's aid from Maj. Gen. John A. McClernand's division, which had camped directly behind Sherman. While such help was welcomed, it could be difficult to distinguish friendly forces coming to Sherman's assistance from enemy troops advancing to Sherman's doom.

Lieutenant Patrick H. White of Barrett's Battery told of how his gunners had just one more step to complete before firing their cannon—pulling the lanyard to send the spark into the barrel of the gun—when the identity of the troops coming toward them came into question: "We saw a line of troops marching with their flank toward us. The men held the lanyards ready to fire but we were not sure whether they were our own or the enemy. Just then Genl Sherman called out dont fire those are our own men, at that moment they wheeled into line, when we saw the rebel flag (of) the 11th La. Tigers. Then we gave them the contents of our guns. I called to the men to doble shot their pieces." The orders to "double shot" the guns meant that the cannon were loaded with not just one round of short-range canister but two rounds—a practice typically reserved for the most desperate situations when the enemy was within 100 yards of the guns.

The 11th Louisiana was from Maj. Gen. Leonidas

The Union line at Shiloh Church had held on for as long as it could before it became obvious to Lt. Patrick H. White of Barrett's Battery that it was time for them to go: "I knew it was time to retreat, as we saw our troops falling back on the right and left. I was preparing to do so when an order came from General Sherman to retire immediately." (gam)

Polk's corps in the third wave of Confederates to pound Sherman's line while his division received minimal Union reinforcements. By 10:00 a.m., Sherman could no longer hold his initial position around the church, and gave the order to retreat. His next position was around the crossroads of the Corinth Road with the Hamburg-Purdy Road, about one-quarter mile to the rear of the ridgeline.

Though Sherman had never been convinced that the Confederate army was just outside of his camps until his men actually came under attack, he immediately grasped the severity of the situation. He was decisive in his actions—never unsure of what to do once the shooting began. Sherman was able to redeem his pre-battle mistakes by his superb battle performance, both along the meeting house ridge and in subsequent phases of the battle.

At Shiloh Church

Across the Corinth Road to your left is a reproduction of the Shiloh Meeting House as well as the modern Shiloh Methodist Church on the site of the original meeting house.

From the orientation station, walk behind you toward

the cemetery until you can easily walk up the bank near the cannon and then walk back in the direction of the orientation station. Locate the trail through the woods to your right front. Carefully watch your footing, as the trail contains several large roots, rocks, and bricks.

Where the trail enters into a small field, stop at the 2nd Tennessee monument in front of you.

Leading the 2nd Tennessee on that April 6 morning was Col. William B. "Old Grits" Bate. Soon the air around them was full of bullets. A typical bullet used during the war was invented in 1849 by a French army officer named Claude-Etienne Minié—the men on both sides called the rifled musket projectile the "minie ball." Sergeant Robert D. Smith summarized the fight of the 2nd Tennessee: "The enemy poured such a destructive fire upon our ranks that we were unable to stand it. Major Doak was killed the first round, having been shot with nine minnie balls. His horse was killed at the same time. Our men fell back a short distance, when Col. Bate rallied them for another charge. We almost went as far this time as we did the first, but were compelled to retreat again."

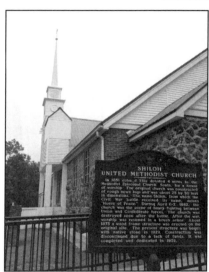

Shiloh United Methodist Church remains an active congregation. (cm)

Colonel Bate, along with four members of his family, were all struck down—killed or wounded—in a short period of time. In one of the initial attacks, the colonel's younger brother, Capt. Humphry Bate, was mortally wounded right in front of him.

Stand at the 2nd Tennessee monument facing downhill. The field in front of you extended 200 yards down the hill at the time of the battle. About another 20 yards from the edge of the field was the East Branch, and running parallel to it a few yards farther was the Shiloh Branch. To your left front, on the other side of both streams, lies Rea Field.

Turn around and walk to the 70th Ohio monument to the left of the trail. Stand beside the 70th Ohio monument facing the 2nd Tennessee monument.

William B. Bate, a 35-year-old former lieutenant in the Mexican War, would become a Confederate general in large part due to his bravery at Shiloh. The colonel was in the act of lighting a cigar when he watched his brother die, and he could never light another cigar for the rest of his life— from that point on, he only chewed on his cigars. (usmi)

Colonel Joseph R. Cockerill commanded the 70th Ohio regiment posted here. The movie at the visitor center features the battle account of his 16-year-old son, John A. Cockerill, a musician in the 24th Ohio. Although not in his father's unit or even in his father's army—since the 24th Ohio was in Buell's Army of the Ohio—John obtained permission to stay with his father while recovering from an illness and, thus, found himself on the front lines in the battle of Shiloh.

Continue following the trail back and stop at the cannon and monument for Barrett's Illinois Battery. Barrett's Battery was positioned just behind the Shiloh Church orientation station. Face the direction the cannon are pointing. The artillerymen near the crest of the hill played a critical role in holding back the Confederate assaults and were hotly engaged. "After a heavy volley (which wounded several of our horses)," wrote one of Barrett's gunners, the Confederate infantry "dashed across the ravine and right up the hill at us." Rounds of canister repulsed the Confederate attack.

When Sherman pulled out from this position, Barrett's gunners were the last to leave as they were assigned the rear guard, holding off the Confederates as long as possible to buy time for the remainder of the division to reform.

Along the way to the next tour stop, be sure to observe the streams and floodplain at the bottom of the hill, which created the swamp that Confederates were forced to negotiate before encountering Sherman's men. Look carefully and notice that you will be crossing two bridges in quick succession over first the East Branch and then Shiloh Branch.

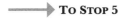 **TO STOP 5**

From Shiloh Church, continue down the road for 0.25 mile. Turn left onto Peabody Road. Drive 0.2 mile and turn left into the parking area for Rea Field.

As the Confederates moved against the Union position, they first encountered the swollen Shiloh Branch (a few yards south of this photograph) and the East Branch. "A worse place could not have been selected for our men to go through, wading creeks, going through thick underbrush & swamp land in mud & water up to our waste [sic]," complained a member of Cleburne's brigade. A short distance beyond the steams, at about 8:00 am, the Confederates stumbled upon Sherman's men. (gam)

Rea Field

CHAPTER FOUR

April 6, 1862—early to mid-morning

As Sherman straddled the Corinth Road at Shiloh Meeting House, his troops east of the road consisted of one brigade commanded by Col. Jesse Hildebrand, a former sheriff, supported by Waterhouse's artillery. Even though Sherman supposedly instructed all of Hildebrand's units to go into camp north of East Branch—using the stream as a barrier in case of the seemingly improbable Confederate attack—one rogue regiment did not heed that directive.

The 53rd Ohio bivouacked in Rea Field south of the East Branch, which doubled as a water source for the troops. The Ohioans apparently camped here because the location afforded easier access to the drinking water at Rea Spring.

Their disregard of camping instructions was not the only aspect of that regiment to annoy Sherman. Colonel Jesse J. Appler, commander of the 53rd Ohio, was one of the officers who inundated Sherman with warnings of the Confederate presence outside of the Union camps. Appler had worked as an auditor and a probate judge in Portsmouth, Ohio, before the war, and he once served as a company commander in the Ohio militia.

Sherman felt contempt for volunteer and militia officers like Appler, and the general seems to have spent little time trying to coach his field grade officers in their proper duties. Instead, Sherman seemed to delight in making Appler the butt of his jokes.

At about 4:00 p.m. on April 5—a time when the entire Confederate army was in position and poised for attack but stalled by deepening twilight—one of Appler's officers thought that he observed mounted Confederates at the south end of Rea Field. Appler responded appropriately by sending a patrol to investigate, and the patrol was fired upon by "what appeared to be a picket line of men in butternut

The opportunity for easy access to drinking water at Rea Spring understandably tempted the 53rd Ohio to set up camp near the spring. It was, however, the only unit to erect its tents south of the stream, while the rest of the army was north of it, placing the 53rd Ohio in arguably the most vulnerable bivouac of any unit in the entire Union army. (gam)

clothes." (Though gray is commonly recognized as the color of Confederate uniforms, the husks of a type of walnut called the butternut proved to be a readily accessible home-made dye, enabling the South to produce light brown uniforms called "butternut," which were very frequently worn by Confederate soldiers.)

As this image shows, the view from Waterhouse's artillery position, posted just east of Shiloh Church, looking across Rea Field, was more expansive than the current view. The wartime field extended some 900 yards in length. (bl)

Appler responded fittingly by calling upon his regiment to fall in and by sending his quartermaster, Lt. Joseph W. Fulton, to inform Sherman of the threat. The quartermaster returned as the command was assembling and announced the general's reply so that all could hear: "Colonel Appler, General Sherman says: 'Take your damned regiment to Ohio. There is no enemy nearer than Corinth!'" The troops had a great laugh at the expense of their commanding officer, and fell out of ranks—before being ordered by Appler to do so.

The next morning, Appler sent a mere 16-man body of troops to keep watch on the south end of Rea Field. When the detail reported the enemy in sizeable numbers, Appler decided to seek confirmation before alerting his superiors. That corroboration came in the form of a soldier from the 25th Missouri—part of Prentiss's neighboring division—who passed through the camp of the 53rd Ohio on his way to the rear seeking medical attention for his bloody arm. The wounded soldier admonished Appler's men: "Get into line; the Rebels are coming!" That was enough evidence for Appler.

*   *   *

Shortly after 6:00 a.m., the long roll sounded—a sustained roll of the drum calling the regiment to fall into line in front of their camp, where they faced west (see Map 7 on page 32 for positions in this chapter). Quartermaster Fulton was once again sent to Sherman's division headquarters. The quartermaster returned with another derisive comment from Sherman. Rather than repeat it so all could hear as he had done the night before, Fulton showed more tact on this morning. He leaned over toward the colonel and in a low tone meant only for Appler's ears said, "General Sherman says you must be badly scared over there." Appler kept his troops in position, wheeling his command to face south, the direction from which his pickets reported, "The rebels out there are thicker than fleas on a dog's back."

No sooner had the regiment moved into position oriented to the south when Adj. Ephraim C. Dawes looked to the west—the direction the regiment had been facing only moments before—and observed yet another startling development. "The sun had arisen in a clear sky, and the bright gun barrels of the advancing line shone through the green leaves," as Dawes spotted the arrival of Cleburne's Confederates advancing astride the Corinth Road to the west of Rea Field.

Modern Rea Field is only about 330 yards from north to south. (gam)

When Cleburne's six regiments encountered the Shiloh Branch and East Branch swamp, two right regiments broke off from the rest and veered east. They advanced into Rea Field, heading straight for the most vulnerable part of the 53rd Ohio's line—the very end or flank. "The Confederate line of battle," Dawes detected, was "apparently within musket shot, and moving directly toward our right flank."

Dawes alerted Appler, "Colonel, look to the right!"

"This is no place for us," Appler thought out loud.

Appler withdrew through the camp to a position at the edge of the woods on the eastern side of the field, once again facing west. The regiment also moved out of the field of fire of Hildebrand's other regiments and Waterhouse's Battery north of Rea Field. Confederates moving into the 53rd Ohio camps would be subjected to a crossfire.

About 7:00 a.m., Sherman rode out to a high point of Rea Field near the 53rd Ohio camp to determine the situation for himself. The general was looking through his field glasses at some Confederates marching across the southern end of Rea Field. While studying this movement, the skirmish line of Cleburne's brigade suddenly emerged from the western edge of the field, approaching Sherman from the side. "General, look to your right," Lt. Eustace H. Ball warned.

"My God, we are attacked!" Sherman exclaimed, as shots rang out from the Confederate muskets.

Smoothbore rounds of buck and ball—a large round ball the caliber of the weapon supplemented with three small buck shot packed together in one round—flew in the direction of Sherman and the group around him. A ball struck Thomas D. Holliday, part of Sherman's cavalry escort, who fell dead by Sherman's side. The general was struck in the hand by a buck shot. Sherman wheeled his horse and dashed by the colonel he had scoffed at before. "Appler, hold our position; I will support you," Sherman promised.

*   *   *

The two regiments making up the right wing of Cleburne entered Rea Field, continuing toward the 53rd Ohio. The 6th Mississippi held the left, advancing on the higher ground closest to the East Branch. The 23rd

Tennessee was on the right. Initially the Confederates "moved as quietly and steadily as on dress parade, a magnificent sight," according to one Ohio soldier.

Advancing through the tents of the 53rd Ohio camp, however, broke up the shoulder-to-shoulder formations that the Mississippians and Tennesseans tried to maintain in their assault. The Ohioans took advantage of the fragmented line silhouetted against the white tents and poured volleys into the Confederates, easily repulsing the first attack. The muzzle-loading weapons that Civil War soldiers fired took about 20-30 seconds to load. "We fired 4 times"—meaning the first attack may have lasted only a couple of minutes—"and killed fifty within the limits of our camp, for we buried them ourselves on Tuesday," explained one of the Ohio soldiers. In addition to the infantry fire from the Buckeyes in front of the Confederates, Union artillery north of East Branch delivered a devastating flanking fire down the enemy line as well.

As Appler withdrew from his brief position where the monument now stands to his position on the east edge of Rea Field, he passed through his camps. Appler ordered "Sick men to the rear." With their new position facing the camp, Appler expected the regiment to soon be firing into their tents, and the non-combatants had to abandon the camp for their own safety. (gam)

The 6th Mississippi attacked again, this time without the aid of the shaken Tennesseans, and when repulsed, regrouped and assaulted a third time. The casualties of the 6th Mississippi probably represent the greatest percentage loss of any Confederate regiment at Shiloh. Though the numbers do not appear to be exact, it has been reported that the regiment lost 300 of its 425 men, a staggering loss in killed and wounded reaching 70.5%.

Although the 53rd Ohio had held its ground with relative ease, something startled Appler. "Retreat and save yourselves," the colonel implored his men. The degree of panic that Appler displayed was unwarranted. Appler had plenty of time to give the proper orders for an organized withdrawal. Instead, most of the regiment fell back pell-mell until a portion of it rallied on the rest

of Hildebrand's brigade east of the church. When in that position, Appler again became rattled and "literally ran away," according to Dawes.

Though Col. Jesse Appler had irritated Sherman by inundating him with warnings of the Confederate presence, his claims proved correct. Otherwise, Appler proved unfit for command and was dismissed from the army on April 18. Even so, one cannot help but feel sympathy for Appler and the numerous similar officers placed in positions far above their training or abilities, men who likewise struggled in their first battle. At the same time, one should reasonably be amazed at how others with similar backgrounds performed so admirably.

*   *   *

It became obvious that the Confederates were not going to make any progress on Sherman's front until they drove Waterhouse's artillery from its position, from which it was raking Rea Field. Striking on its left flank held the best prospect of Southern success. The assignment fell to Col. Alfred J. Vaughan, commanding the 13th Tennessee in Col. Robert M. Russell's brigade. Division commander Brig. Gen. Charles Clark called out to Vaughan, "Can you take that battery yonder, which is annoying our troops so much?" "We can take it," Vaughn curtly replied.

As the 13th Tennessee set out on its mission to neutralize Waterhouse, it discovered firsthand the devastation of the Illinois battery's fire. "As we emerged from behind the tents, right into the plain view of the enemy, whom we could not see," complained Capt. Samuel R. Latta, "they opened

This is one of five Confederate burial trenches identified and marked within the boundaries of the Shiloh National Military Park. The search throughout a twelve-square-mile area directed by Edmund B. Whitman begun in 1866 discovered eleven or twelve Confederate burial trenches. By the time the commission that created the park was established, only nine trenches could be located. Six or seven similar burial plots have been lost to history. (gam)

Likely after Polk's Battery abandoned this position, the 11th Louisiana in Russell's brigade attacked—possibly over this ground. The regiment's Lt. John Crowly had returned from sick leave four days before the battle, recuperating from the amputation of his right arm from a wound suffered in the November 7, 1861, battle of Belmont, Missouri. While attacking Sherman's line, Crowley was hit in his left arm by a fragment of artillery shrapnel and lost that arm as well. (gam)

When Leonidas Polk's corps was committed to the battle, all three of the Confederate corps thus far engaged became intermingled. Polk and Bragg then initiated the practice of each corps commander taking control of a particular sector of the field, regardless of whether or not those troops belonged to their own corps. Polk thenceforth took command of the region astride the Corinth Road, including Rea Field and Shiloh Church. (loc)

upon us with grape, and canister, and musketry and our men fell back at once into the woods."

But by 9:30 a.m., the 13th Tennessee had gained the flank of Hildebrand's line and directly threatened Waterhouse's Battery. Major Benjamin Fearing of the 77th Ohio, positioned at the church, observed, "The left gave way and the devils took a battery and planted their flag directly on our left."

By 10:00 a.m., Sherman had no choice but to retire after nearly three hours of resistance. The cannon were limbering up to escape, when Capt. Allen C. Waterhouse, the 28-year old battery commander, was wounded in the leg. About 100 yards farther to the rear, the battery was ordered to drop trail and open fire again. There, three of their guns were captured.

Confederates noted the carnage of the terrible fight as they occupied Sherman's former position. "The ground was strewn with the dead of the enemy and our own, mangled in every conceivable way," wrote Captain Latta. "A federal soldier was laying dead, and beside him a beautiful dog who would suffer no one to approach his dead master." Latta's commanding officer, Colonel Vaughan, probably witnessed the same scene when he described a "pointer dog" guarding the body of its owner.

The cost had been high, but the Confederates had pried Sherman out of his Shiloh Church position and would try to drive him into the Owl Creek swamps.

At Rea Field

Although the field and spring here have come to be more commonly spelled "Rhea," the family that settled here distinctly spelled their name "Rea."

At the end of the parking lot closest to the entrance, at a gap in the stone wall, a trail leads downhill to East Branch and Rea Spring (stop 5A). From the stream, you can see cannon, near the top of the hill on the other side of East Branch, that mark the position of Waterhouse's Battery E, 1st Illinois Artillery, which was posted in an open wood where it could fire across Rea Field.

From your vantage point, the Shiloh Meeting House was about 300 yards to the left and behind Waterhouse's position.

Walk back to the parking lot and down the entrance lane. Cross over Peabody Road to the trail marked "Confederate Burials 0.1 mi." Continue down the trail to the black marker shaped like a tent on the left side of the trail marking the camp of the 53rd Ohio (stop 5B). In 1862, when facing the direction of the current marker for the 53rd Ohio camps, rows of tents would have stretched out in front of you. The marker is positioned at the "color line"—a place in front of the camp where the flag or "colors" would have been posted, and where the troops would have fallen into formation. Rea Field extended another 700 yards to the south from the center of the 53rd Ohio camp; the field is much smaller today than it was at the time of the battle.

Face right and look south down the trail as it leads to a Confederate burial trench near the bottom of the hill. This is one of the five Confederate burial trenches that has been located and marked.

From the trail going toward the Confederate burial trench, you can walk to the monument (to your left front) marking the position where Appler moved the 53rd Ohio to face south after it had initially formed up in front of its camp (stop 5C).

Walk back toward the parking lot. Just before reaching Peabody Road, stop at the blue tablet and cannon for a section (two guns) of Waterhouse's Battery to the left of the trail (stop 5D). Face west, the direction that the cannon are pointing.

By the time Sherman departed Rea Field with his hand slightly wounded, a two-gun section of Waterhouse's Battery of six cannon had already joined the 53rd Ohio. The isolated position south of East Branch was not a favorable one for artillery, and after firing a very short time—Dawes indicated that each gun fired only one shot—

Patrick Cleburne was on the right of his brigade and was with his two regiments in Rea Field when their first attack was thrown back. "Boys, do not be discouraged," he shouted reassuringly. "That was not the first charge that was ever repulsed." Cleburne was destined to be one of the best division commanders in all of Confederate service. (loc)

While the monument honors all troops from the state that fought at Shiloh, the figures and flag represent the 6th Mississippi of Cleburne's brigade in Hardee's corps, which fought at this location. They carried the "Hardee pattern battle flag," as did most regiments in that corps, which was a blue flag with a white full moon in the middle. (gam)

they returned to the higher ground to the north with the rest of the battery. The 53rd Ohio would have to defend the middle of Rea Field on its own.

Even so, the artillery and infantry on the north side of the stream in north Rea Field played a significant role in the fighting. Perhaps at the same time that Sherman was watching Confederates crossing the south end of the field, his division artillery chief, Ezra Taylor, observed troops in that same location "bearing aloft, as I supposed, the American flag, and their men and officers wearing uniforms so similar to ours, that I hesitated to open fire on them." Not until the next regiment crossed the field comprised of "troops who wore a uniform not to be mistaken" did Taylor order Waterhouse to open fire at about 7:30 a.m.

Turn around to face east, placing the cannon and tablet behind you. You now face the general direction of the initial Confederate attacks into Rea Field and are in the vicinity where the 6th Mississippi most likely fought. Ahead of you at the tree line was the position of the 53rd Ohio.

Turn back around and walk west, parallel to Peabody Road, to the cannon by the red tablet for Polk's Battery (stop 5E). Face north, the direction the cannon are pointing.

The first wave in the Confederate attack had splintered before it reached the Union camps. Then as the second Confederate line under Bragg surged forward about 8:30 a.m. and the third column under Polk emerged on the scene about 9:00 a.m., the troops from all three corps intermingled.

While the intermixing of infantry brigades was certainly detrimental to the Confederate army, the artillery adapted quite well. Batteries accompanying the brigades in this sector joined together to form an impressive mass of some twenty-four pieces of artillery. Eighteen were aligned about one-half mile from Sherman's line while another battery under Capt. Marshall Polk, set up in Rea Field where you now stand, a mere 300 yards from Hildebrand's line. Polk's gunners were too far in advance of the rest of the Confederate artillery, and Union batteries pummeled the gray artillery. The battery commander, Polk, was wounded in the leg and five of its six cannon knocked out of action.

Cross Peabody Road and, on your way to your vehicle, notice the impressive Mississippi monument in the island between Peabody Road and the parking lot.

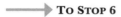 **TO STOP 6**

Exit the parking lot and turn right on Peabody Road. Drive 0.2 mile and turn left on Corinth Road. Drive 0.6 mile to a 90-degree bend in the road. Park in the pull-off on the right side of the road. Walk to the orientation station (stop 6A).

First Contact

CHAPTER FIVE

April 6, 1862—early morning

Like Colonel Appler, Col. Everett Peabody was stationed on the outskirts of the Union camp, recognized the signs of the nearby Confederate buildup, was unable to convince his division commander to heed his warning, and couldn't sleep the night before the battle. But unlike Appler, Peabody was the senior colonel in the brigade, with the authority to act upon his assessment. He also had the all-important military experience prior to the Civil War.

The 31-year-old, Massachusetts-born, Harvard-educated Peabody had been wounded and captured along with the rest of the Union garrison in the battle of Lexington, Missouri, seven months before Shiloh. While both of the divisions camped on the outskirts of the Union bivouac were essentially green troops, Peabody's now-reconstituted Lexington regiment, the 25th Missouri, was an exception among them.

During the pre-dawn hours of April 6, Peabody sent a patrol out to gather the latest information on whatever Confederate force was in front of his camp. Peabody made a good choice in selecting Maj. James E. Powell for this mission. Powell was an experienced army officer who was also skeptical of the prevailing attitude at division headquarters that the Confederates were still at Corinth.

Powell was directed to gather 250 men from the 25th Missouri and 12th Michigan to comprise a 3:00 a.m. reconnoitering party. The five companies proceeded down an old wagon-wheel-rutted lane now called "Reconnoitering Road." They formed in three columns—one in the road, the other two through the woods on either side of the road.

As Powell's band of soldiers entered Seay Field, they encountered some of Brewer's Alabama Cavalry and three warning shots rang out before the horsemen galloped away.

In the early morning hours of April 6, 1862, Fraley Field saw the opening shots of what would become the bloodiest battle in American history to date. (cm)

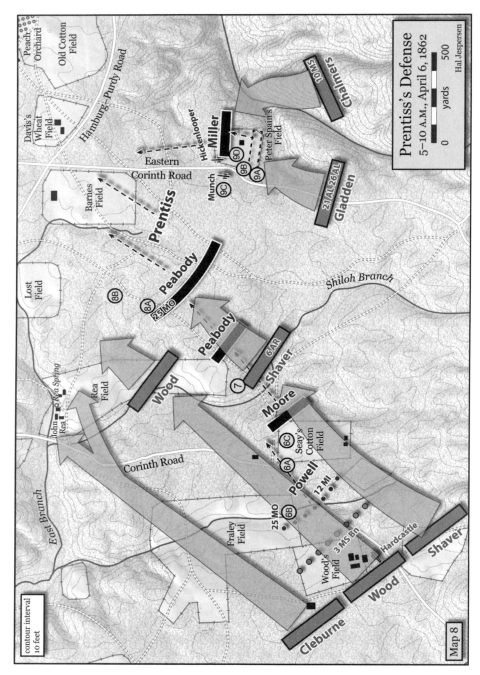

PRENTISS'S DEFENSE—Col. Everett Peabody, one of Gen. Benjamin M. Prentiss's subordinates, discovered the Confederates during a pre-dawn reconnoiter and grudgingly gave ground until the battle reached the outskirts of their camp. Terrain did not aid in slowing down the Confederates, as had been the case on the edge of Sherman's camp. Prentiss's men were overwhelmed and in retreat about 9:00 a.m.

A short distance after leaving Seay Field, the Union patrol crossed the Corinth Road.

Here, Powell decided it was time to abandon the three-column formation in favor of spreading out into a thin skirmish line. A further advance in skirmish line formation also required at least a minimal amount of light. When the first few rays of dawn broke through the darkness, the scouting mission resumed, pressing forward on both sides of the Corinth Road.

After advancing astride the Corinth Road about 100 yards, the right end of the reconnoitering party—men from the 25th Missouri—entered the 40-acre John C. Fraley cotton field. The next layer in the security of the Confederate army after the cavalry pickets in Seay Field were infantry pickets in Fraley Field. By the time the Union reconnoitering party reached the middle of Fraley Field, Powell's soldiers would discover that Confederate resistance was about to change.

Waiting in place on the far side of the field was Maj. Aaron B. Hardcastle's 3rd Mississippi Battalion of 280 men, also in skirmish line. Powell's troops could see Hardcastle's kneeling men in the dim light and opened fire. The Confederates shot back. About 4:55 a.m., the battle of Shiloh had begun. Word of the encounter was sent back to Peabody, and some 530 men—the total of the men on both sides—continued skirmishing for the next hour.

Powell's orders were not only to "drive in the guard" but to also "develop the force, hold the ground as long as possible, then fall back." Powell tried to push forward to discover just what was beyond the Confederate skirmish line, but Hardcastle would not budge. Like Powell, Hardcastle was a regular army officer when the war broke out and did his job well.

Hardcastle's skirmish line was a few hundred yards in front of Hardee's main battle line. The skirmish line was in place, first, to make sure that the main line would be warned in advance of an approach by the enemy and, second, to stop any enemy probes from learning the full extent of the Confederate build-up behind the line—and as yet, Powell's mid-westerners could not determine the might of the force behind the Mississippians.

As the troops moved closer together, as daylight improved visibility, and as the excited men settled down, bullets hit their mark with more regularity; casualties began to trickle to the rear. After an hour of skirmishing, it appeared to Powell that a Confederate cavalry force was moving through the woods beyond his left flank, and the time to withdraw had arrived. Then, just as Powell disengaged with the Confederates, he noted that Hardcastle had withdrawn, as well. Soon Powell would discover why.

Everett Peabody and many of his men had been in the 13th Missouri and were part of the Union garrison captured in the September 12-20, 1861, battle of Lexington, Missouri. This unique Civil War battle was fought between Union forces and the Missouri State Guard—not Confederate troops. After a prisoner exchange, the regiment was reorganized into the 25th Missouri and fought at Shiloh. (wcnb)

These two small markers are on either side of the trail leading down to the scene of the opening shots of the battle in Fraley Field. Each marker indicates the distance to the initial skirmish line positions for each opposing army. (gam)

Thousands of Confederate soldiers in the first assault wave suddenly spread out across the entirety of Fraley Field for Powell's men to see—yet they observed but a fraction of the massive Confederate attack, as the vast majority of men were still concealed in the woods on either side of the field, as well as the reserves stacked up behind Hardee's front line for nearly two miles.

The time was about 6:30 a.m. The Union reconnoitering party had accomplished its mission, and it was time for it to spread the word of the discovery.

* * *

Even as Powell's band fell back into Seay Field, help was soon on the way. The reinforcements included some of Col. David Moore's 21st Missouri along with men from the 16th Wisconsin. Moore had performed a flawed reconnaissance of his own just the evening before and was confident that his contingency could handle whatever Confederates were heading his way. "We would finish them up in no time," Moore predicted.

Powell knew better. Moore ridiculed Powell for withdrawing in front of what Moore was sure was a small force, yet he ordered all members of Powell's party not to assist their wounded so they could instead augment his force.

Skirmishing that began in Fraley and Seay fields spread into the woods, and Moore soon realized his estimate of the situation was wrong. In the ensuing fight, Moore suffered a leg wound that would require an amputation.

The Confederates rolling toward Seay Field comprised the Arkansas brigade of Col. Robert Shaver. The Confederate army commander saw the fight in the field first-hand, rallying some men who had broken, giving them encouragement as well as bracing them for the close-up fighting he anticipated to

Lt. Col. Humphrey Woodward of the 21st Missouri took command of the troops in Seay Field after Moore was wounded. They eventually took position along both the northern and eastern sides of the field. "The position proved a strong one," in the opinion of Woodward, "and we managed to hold it for upwards of an hour." (gam)

come. "Men of Arkansas! They say you boast of your prowess with the bowie-knife," General Johnston acknowledged. "To-day you wield a nobler weapon—the bayonet. Employ it well."

*　　*　　*

The Union forces withdrew to the next defensible position, and the Confederates pursued. The fight developed into a running battle, with the Union soldiers halting at places where the terrain offered benefits as they withdrew toward their camps. At a ridge about one-quarter mile south of Peabody's camp, the Powell-Moore assemblage was joined by Peabody bringing up the remainder of the 25th Missouri and the 12th Michigan. The combined Union forces made a stand on the ridge from about 7:30-8:00 am. "Looking to the front again," recalled Charles Morton, one of the Missourians advancing with Peabody, "I saw, coming down a gentle slope within easy range the Confederates massed many lines deep."

On the Confederate side, Henry M. Stanley of the 6th Arkansas approached the same body of Union soldiers to which Morton belonged. On getting his first view of the Union soldiers, Stanley wrote, "'There they are!' was no sooner uttered, than we cracked into them with leveled muskets. 'Aim low, men!' commanded Captain Smith. I tried hard to see some living thing to shoot at, for it appeared absurd to be blazing away at shadows. But, still advancing, firing as we moved, I, at last, saw a row of little globes of pearly smoke streaked with crimson, breaking out, with sportive quickness, from a long line of blue figures in front. Simultaneously, there broke upon our ears an appalling crash of sound. . . ."

Morton recalled the banter between the opposing

A native of Wales, Henry Morton Stanley would later become a famed explorer. He is best known for his African expedition and search for Dr. Samuel Livingstone, including the casual manner in which he apparently approached the doctor in 1871: "Dr. Livingstone, I presume?" (lspc)

soldiers: "The 'Johnnies' yelled vociferously 'Bull Run, Bull Run!' and our men shouted back defiance—'Why don't you come on?'" The term "Johnnies" or "Johnny Reb" were nicknames Union soldiers had for the Confederates. The July 21, 1861, battle of Bull Run had ended with many of the Union soldiers fleeing from the field in panic, and the Confederate chant was its prediction that Morton and his comrades would be heading rapidly to the rear as well.

Morton noted the intensity of the fight: "soon our men commenced to fall thick and fast. . . . This position was held until our unsupported right and left were being turned when we fell back from tree to tree, to avert being enveloped. Every step was stubbornly disputed."

Soon the men who had left Prentiss's camps in small numbers either as the reconnoitering party or as its reinforcements would all be reunited along with the regiments that had remained in the camps. Together the full division would make its most substantial stand of the battle.

* * *

Colonel Everett Peabody was certain that he had done the right thing by sending out a pre-dawn reconnoitering party. He was also certain what needed to be done when the sounds of firing from that reinforced party fighting in Seay Field reached his headquarters. But as Peabody prepared to mount his horse and take the balance of his brigade forward, someone rode up who was just as certain that Peabody had made a huge lapse in judgment.

About 7:00 a.m., Gen. Benjamin Prentiss galloped along the line of troops responding to the long roll that Peabody had sounded. The general reined up his horse next to his presumably misguided brigade commander. "Colonel Peabody, I will hold you personally responsible for bringing on this engagement," Prentiss scolded. A confident and contemptuous Peabody exclaimed, "General Prentiss, I am personally responsible for all my official acts."

Peabody rode off with his men to fight the engagement on the ridge one-quarter mile south and soon returned for a stand at his headquarters and an engagement involving the entire division. The other brigade in the division, under Col. Madison Miller, was off to the east, comprising Prentiss's left flank, while Peabody held the right. "With a look of mortified pride but great determination on his handsome face he conjured the men to hold their ground," recalled Charles Morton.

Regiments were allowed to list the names of battles in which they had been engaged upon their colors. Peabody wanted to evoke the memory of the stand the 25th Missouri made against overwhelming odds before they surrendered in their first battle. "Pointing to the words in golden letters

In the initial combat in Seay Field, 43-year-old Capt. Edward Saxe of the 16th Wisconsin has the distinction of being the first Union officer to lose his life in the battle of Shiloh. His grave in the Shiloh National Cemetery is marked with this non-government issued stone. The six members of the Wisconsin Color Bearer prominently buried together in the cemetery also belonged to the 16th Wisconsin. (gam)

on our flag," recalled Morton, "he cried out: 'Lexington, men; Lexington; remember Lexington!'"

Brigadier General Sterling A. M. Wood's Confederate brigade had been under artillery fire from Sherman as it crossed the southern end of Rea Field, but it had otherwise bypassed Sherman, venturing into the gap between the two outlying Union divisions. About 8:15 a.m., Wood emerged on Peabody's right flank, adding weight to that of Shaver's brigade, which had been pressuring the front of portions of Peabody's command from Seay Field all the way to the brigade camp. The combined force was more than the 25th Missouri could handle, and the men were obliged to withdraw.

* * *

With pressure from Shaver on its front and Wood on its right flank, the 25th Missouri was compelled to take a position behind its camps, where tents masked them from enemy view, and trees offered some measure of protection. "The enemy could not dislodge us," Morton explained. "He dared not charge over the comparatively open ground between us, and for the same reason, as well as because of our disorganized condition and his vastly superior numbers, we could not charge him; but we held him at musket range, and expected momentarily support."

The first sign of what seemed to be Union

Various witnesses recall the words between Peabody and Prentiss differently. One recalled Prentiss reprimanding Peabody with the words, "You have brought on an attack for which I am unprepared and I shall hold you responsible," and Peabody predicting, "General, you will soon see that I was not mistaken." Prentiss's report of the battle shamelessly takes credit for actions initiated by the dead Peabody. (gam)

reinforcements was a battery that moved into position off to their left, near the Eastern Corinth Road. But the Missourians were dismayed when the cannon turned on them rather than the enemy. "Even ahead of the deafening reports of the gun came a storm of missiles screaming and shrieking through the air,"—as Morton observed, artillery projectiles travelled faster than the speed of sound—"ripping through the tents, smashing tentpoles, knocking from the trees limbs that rained upon us, tearing up the ground, and raising a blinding dust."

The left end of Prentiss's line had given way, and the battery Morton had observed was a Confederate battery that had commandeered the former Union position. The help that Prentiss's men anticipated from other divisions camped further to the rear would never arrive. It was hopeless for Prentiss's troops to try to save their camps.

Morton reported that a small portion of the 25th Missouri tried to hold on, making a last stand in the far rear of their camp where the officers' tents were pitched. "Here Colonel Peabody's horse passed us, riderless and stirrups flapping in the air," he sadly observed. "We knew our brave and noble Colonel had fallen," Morton concluded. Earlier in the fight, Peabody had been wounded four times—in the neck, torso, hand, and thigh. At about 8:45 a.m., a final mortal wound struck the colonel in the upper lip, exiting the back of his head.

At Fraley Field

From the orientation station near the park tour road, the trail to Fraley Field is just a few yards ahead. (gam)

At the orientation station (stop 6A), notice the grassy roadbed running ahead, which is the continuation of the Corinth Road that you have been travelling along. You are at the intersection of the Corinth Road and an unnamed farm lane from the time of the battle that has since come to be known as "Reconnoitering Road." The Reconnoitering Road is the continuation of the park tour road behind you and to your left, as well as the trail farther to the right of the Corinth roadbed.

Turn around, with your back to the exhibits, and look down the paved portion of Reconnoitering Road. Powell's reconnoitering party advanced toward you during the pre-dawn hours of April 6. The patrol originated from its camp, about three-quarter mile ahead of you. The open area to the right of Reconnoitering Road is Seay Field.

Turn around and take the portion of the Reconnoitering Road, which is now a trail. A small blue marker on the left of the trail and a small red marker on the right mark the trailhead. Follow the trail for about 200 yards to the edge of Fraley Field.

Stop at the orientation station where the trail emerges from the woods (stop 6B). You are in the southeast corner of Fraley Field. About 250 yards ahead of you, just to the left of the trail is a red tablet marking the location of Hardcastle's Confederate troops. Depending upon the crop cover, this may be difficult to see at certain times of the year.

When you return along the trail and reach the paved portion of Reconnoitering Road, continue walking along the road shoulder to the right for about 75 yards. Stop at the road marker for "Reconnoitering Road" and the small black marker for "Seay Field" (stop 6C). You are near the northwest corner of that field.

One of the soldiers who suffered an arm wound in the Fraley fight found his way into the camp of the 53rd Ohio in Rea Field about 6:00 a.m., resulting in Colonel Appler's call for the long roll. Peabody responded to the wounded who returned to his camp by sending another larger body of soldiers to the aid of the reconnoitering party. As Powell's soldiers fell back down the old farm lane toward his camp, that relief party caught up with them near this spot. The blue tablet in Seay Field marks a position for Moore's relief party.

Although the Union soldiers were overwhelmed in this second stand-up fight of the morning, the Confederate assault was slowed and the Southerners forced to engage the Northern army at a point of contact far outside of the Union camps.

Both armies were well served by the veteran majors directing the fighting in Fraley Field. Union Maj. James E. Powell was an immigrant from England, who joined the army after Karankawa Indians killed his wife and two children in Texas in 1843 while he was absent from home on a hunting trip. He remarried, and his 12-year-old son, also named James, was in camp with him at Shiloh. Confederate Maj. Aaron B. Hardcastle had been a lieutenant in the U.S. army at the outbreak of the Civil War and had traveled along with A. S. Johnston from their posts in California to Tennessee, offering their services to the Confederacy. (gam)

 **TO STOP 7**

Drive down Reconnoitering Road 0.4 mile to the tour stop for "Confederates Gain Ground."

On the Ridge: "Confederates Gain Ground"

Recent studies have challenged previously held views that the newer-style rifled muskets gave soldiers using them a distinct advantage over those with older smoothbore muskets. Apparently, troops yielding both types of weapons typically opened their initial fire upon the enemy at a range of only about 100 yards. This is a view from the ridge occupied by Shaver's Confederate brigade as they looked across a ravine to the ridge held by a portion of Peabody's Union brigade—a distance of about 100 yards. (gam)

Walk over to the left road shoulder—the opposite side of the road from the orientation station. Look ahead, across the ravine to the blue marker on the next ridge. You are now on the ridge that Confederate soldiers in Shavers's Arkansas brigade occupied when they were shooting at Peabody's Union troops on that ridge across the ravine. This tour stop provides a good idea of just how close opposing battle lines of Civil War soldiers often were while engaged in a fire fight.

Charles Morton, one of the Missourians advancing with Peabody, described the open forest here as a "heavy oak timber, pretty free from underbrush." Most of the woods of the Shiloh battlefield were mature forests. Livestock roamed the woods eating acorns and nuts on the ground, and otherwise kept down the amount of undergrowth. Therefore, the soldiers who fought at Shiloh generally could see the enemy through the woods when they were within musket range.

▶ To Stop 8

Drive 0.3 mile to a "T" intersection. Turn right, then immediately pull off to the left and park. Walk back past the road intersection to the blue tablet for the 25th Missouri (stop 8A).

At Peabody's Camp

Peabody was scolded by Prentiss as he formed his men here. After advancing to meet the Confederates, Peabody's men soon fell back to this line and then through their camp.

Beyond the camp tablet for the 25th Missouri stands a monument with the upright cannon and the four small cannonball stacks at each corner (stop 8B). This is one of five mortuary monuments in the park, each marking the location where the commander of a brigade (or larger body of troops) was mortally wounded in the battle. The star on top of one of the cannonball pyramids indicates that this monument also marks the brigade headquarters. Peabody's headquarters was in the rear of the 25th Missouri camps, so the area you just walked through from the 25th Missouri camp tablet to the mortuary monument would have contained rows of tents at the time of the battle.

With Prentiss unwilling to give Peabody credit for positively discovering the Confederates and alerting the Union army, and with the dead colonel unable to proffer his true role in the battle, Everett Peabody was not immediately heralded as a hero of the battle of Shiloh. Prentiss would consider his own part in the next phase of the battle along the Sunken Road to be the key to saving the Union army at Shiloh —a view that was prominently endorsed as valid for many decades.

But recently, Peabody's reactions to the information of an enemy presence, his leadership in sending out an unauthorized reconnaissance on the morning of the battle, and his bravery in directing the tactical actions in front of his camp to slow the Confederate assault have been widely recognized as critically impacting the battle. Peabody gave other Union forces the opportunity to better prepare for the onslaught and thus provided immense service to the Union war effort.

"[W]e were the first to take the medicine, and we got it in heavy doses," wrote Lt. James Newhard of the 25th Missouri, who added that his regiment and division "were badly handled from the start." (gam)

⟶ TO STOP 9

The next stop contains a slight detour from the park tour route.

Drive 0.4 mile and turn right onto the Eastern Corinth Road. Drive 0.1 mile to the Gladden mortuary monument (similar to the monument you just visited where Peabody was killed). Just past the Gladden monument pull off to the left, where a single parking space is located. If the parking space is occupied, it is permissible to park on the road shoulder.

Into the Hornet's Nest

CHAPTER SIX

April 6, 1862—early to mid-morning

Benjamin M. Prentiss was a 42-year-old lawyer with both local militia and Mexican War experience, though his run for Congress on the Republican ticket in 1860 was likely a factor in his rise to general. Of Prentiss's two brigades, Peabody bivouacked west of the Eastern Corinth Road, and Miller went into camp to the east, in the woods north of Spain's Field.

Madison Miller was 51-year-old former railroad executive and politician, who was also a veteran of the Mexican War, wounded at battle of Buena Vista. Shortly after chastising Peabody, but nonetheless accepting that a fight was heading his way, Prentiss found Miller and his staff sitting down to breakfast. "Colonel Miller, get out your brigade!" the division commander ordered. "They are fighting on the right."

Miller directed his men to form line of battle on the north end of Spain's Field, where much of the brigade had an open field of fire in front of them. But Prentiss was displeased with Miller's disposition and ordered him forward to the south side of the field overlooking a small valley making up the headwaters of Locust Grove Branch. Miller reluctantly obeyed (see Map 8 on page 52 for positions in this chapter).

While Miller's men were shifting positions, Gen. Adley H. Gladden's Confederate brigade was heading directly toward them. Like Miller, Gladden was 51 years of age, and had also been wounded in the Mexican War. When it became obvious that the three brigades of Hardee's corps could not adequately cover the front assigned to it, Gladden's brigade from Bragg's second line was ordered to take the extreme right flank in the first line.

Even with the addition of Gladden's brigade to the Confederate front ranks, it did not extend beyond the Union

The Minnesota monument sits at the east edge of the Hornets' Nest. Unlike the more open woods found on most of the Shiloh countryside, the thickets of the Hornets' Nest were dense and exceedingly difficult for soldiers in shoulder-to-shoulder formations to advance through, making it a wonderful obstacle behind which the Union army could establish their new line. Conversely, open fields on either side of the Hornets' Nest provided Union soldiers with a completely opposite type of advantage—the opportunity to effectively fire at attacking Confederates multiple times before they neared the Union position. To Confederates attacking the Sunken Road, each portion of the Union line presented some type of significant challenge. (gam)

left flank as planned. When Gladden was informed that another Confederate brigade was being sent to assist him and extend the line even farther, he apparently considered it a criticism and resented the implication that he needed any help. Gladden imprudently attacked before that help arrived, and thus the initial Confederate attack on Miller's line, at about 8 a.m., was a frontal attack without a flanking component.

During the attack, Gladden was mortally wounded and his men suffered severely. The brigade waivered, and Private Liberty Independence Nixon, in Gladden's 26th Alabama, wrote, "Our Officers ordered us to fall back to a Ravine some 30 or 40 steps in our rear."

*   *   *

South Carolina native Adley Gladden was a cotton broker and postmaster who resided in New Orleans when the war broke out. His initial service was under Braxton Bragg in Pensacola, Florida. The normally hard-to-please Bragg was profuse in his praise of Gladden over the first six months of the war. (loc)

Describing the time Gladden's men spent regrouping in the ravine following the brigade's initial repulse, Liberty Nixon wrote, "We only Stayed here a few minutes when we were ordered to charge which we did with a shout. We ran up near enough to be certain that our balls would reach them. We than fired a tremendous volley which seemed to have a considerable effect on them. . . . They gave way in great discord."

The "shout" of Nixon and his comrades did not go unnoticed by the Union soldiers. Captain Andrew Hickenlooper of the 5th Ohio Battery described it as "a 'rebel yell' that caused an involuntary thrill of terror to pass like an electric shock though even the bravest hearts."

About the time that Gladden's initial attack was repulsed, Prentiss had decided to reposition his troops, withdrawing them to the north side of the field and the color line of Miller's camps. It may be that Prentiss realized the wisdom in Miller's initial position, or he might have wanted to adjust Miller's line for fear that Peabody could not hold the right of the division position. This second Confederate attack hurried them along.

As Gladden's brigade again applied pressure to Miller's front, another Confederate brigade, under Brig. Gen. James R. Chalmers, joined the fray. Chalmers not only gave the Confederates an advantage in numbers in Spain's Field, but also enabled them to strike Miller's left flank. Colonel Robert A. Smith, commanding the 10th Mississippi, boasted that his command "commenced firing and with a loud cheer rushed upon the foe," and the Union left collapsed about 9:00 a.m.

"Realizing the hopelessness of our position," lamented Hickenlooper, "I have but time to order 'Limber to the rear,' when there comes a crashing volley, that sweeps our front as with a scythe." As the infantry supports melted away, battery horses to haul off the guns went down. The battery was able to escape with only four of its six guns.

Confederates rushed into the abandoned Union camps, where they were excited by the plethora of food and goods while also stunned by the horrors they found: "I walked around to look at the dead and wounded which lay thick over the camp ground," wrote Nixon, "They were mangled in every conceivable form."

Confederate troops, who had completed a march that lasted longer than the rations they had been issued, were hungry and helped themselves to Union breakfasts arrayed on tables or cooking on the fires. Green troops who may have thought that they had already won the battle by driving the enemy out of their camps took to plunder. Confederate officers tried to get their men to fall back into line.

Even army commander Johnston got involved in turning the Confederates out of the Union camps. Johnston was in the camp of the 18th Wisconsin, east of Spain's Field, when he spotted a Confederate officer come out of a tent with about as much loot as he could carry. "None of that, sir," Johnston scolded, "we are not here for plunder!" Then showing some empathy for what was probably a volunteer officer still learning his responsibilities, and perhaps not wanting to humiliate the officer in front of his men, Johnston softened his reprimand. Reaching down to a camp table, the army commander grabbed a small tin cup and announced, "Let this be my share of the spoils today."

Artilleryman William Christie of Munch's Battery indicated that the enemy was only about 100 yards away when they first went into position—probably the location of this cannon. After the infantry supports gave way, Christie admitted "we had to get out of that place fast as we could" and they again went into battery a short distance further to the rear. (gam)

In relatively short order, the Confederates who had engaged in plunder were out of the camps, back in line, and ready to return to the fight. Most were redirected to the west—toward McClernand's camps and Sherman's line near the meeting house—in conjunction with Johnston's plan to turn the Union left flank and push the enemy into the swamps of Owl Creek. When Chalmers drove in Miller's left flank in Spain's Field, Johnston may have believed that he had caved in the left flank of the entire Union army.

No sooner had that move to the west begun, however, than new intelligence about Union troop positions reached Johnston while he was still in the Spain's Field sector. Captain Samuel H. Lockett, of Bragg's staff, observed a sizeable Union force less than a mile farther east of the field, guarding the Hamburg-Savannah Road crossing of Lick Creek near the Tennessee River.

Johnston seemed to immediately appreciate the

significance of this force in relation to his battle plan. Turning the Union left flank was paramount to the

effectiveness of the design, and it was apparently clear to Johnston at that moment that Prentiss did not represent the left of the army. Johnston promptly pulled two brigades from the movement toward the log church and redirected them to the Lick Creek crossing. Johnston also called for his reserve corps to add its weight to the fight to take place on the far Confederate right.

* * *

Sgt. George Dixon in Gladden's 21st Alabama carried a $20 gold piece in the pocket of his pantaloons during the battle—a good luck charm from his sweetheart Queenie Bennett. The coin absorbed the impact of a bullet that struck him, and he later had it inscribed: "Shiloh April 6, 1862 My Life Preserver G.E.D." Dixon went on to become a lieutenant and the commander of the submarine H. L. *Hunley*. On February 17, 1864, the *Hunley* sank to the bottom of Charleston Harbor after successfully sinking a Union ship. When the sub was raised 137 years later, the coin that Queenie had presented to Dixon (below) was found to be with him still! (gam)(cm)

As Prentiss retreated toward the Union rear, he met with reinforcements dispatched to help his division. Though this help arrived too late to save their camps, those of Prentiss's men who were not panic stricken were able to rally because of the fresh soldiers coming to their aid. The amalgamation of Prentiss's broken troops with orderly reinforcements happened along the Eastern Corinth Road at the point where a simple road trace crossed it on the top of a thickly wooded knoll. The slightly eroded trace would eventually come to be known as the "Sunken Road" (see Map 11 on page 84 for Sunken Road positions).

One of the yet-to-be engaged divisions meeting Prentiss at the Sunken Road was commanded by Brig. Gen. William H. L. Wallace. Soon an additional division arrived from the rear under Brig. Gen. Stephen Hurlbut. Men from these two divisions noted the rattled condition of both Prentiss and his men. The men making up the remnant of Prentiss's division "seemed to be much frightened," wrote B. F. Thomas of Wallace's 14th Iowa. "They were scattered like skirmishers and said the rebels were coming in heavy columns." Hugh Reed in Hurlbut's 44th Indiana reported finding the general himself disheveled: Prentiss was "clamoring for he knew not what—the line to be pushed forward to his former position, etc. He was as demoralized as his troops."

Rather than try to retake Prentiss's camps, the troops wisely settled into position along the Sunken Road and prepared for the inevitable Confederate approach. The Sunken Road became the centerpiece of the second phase of the battle, lasting from about 10:00 a.m. to 6:00 p.m.

Wallace's men took up a position along or behind the Sunken Road predominantly north of the Eastern Corinth Road. Much of Wallace's command looked over the open Duncan Field, but the left of the line fronted the thickets on the little hill.

To the south of Wallace came the vestiges of Prentiss's division, which were joined by one of the new regiments just assigned to the division—the 23rd Missouri—which by itself doubled the size of Prentiss's command to 1,100 men. Prentiss small band of soldiers were completely posted in the woods.

Hurlbut's troops occupied the wooded roadway on Prentiss's left and followed it to a peach orchard and an old cotton field. Together the three divisions numbered some 11,000 men, supported by 38 cannon, occupying more than one-half mile of the Sunken Road. The 600-yard densely wooded portion of the road in the center would become known by the ominous name of the "Hornets' Nest."

At Spain Field

Advance warning and favorable terrain—these were the key elements that determined the degree to which the outlying Union divisions made substantial stands in front of their camps rather than being attacked in their tents, as the opening of the battle of Shiloh has sometimes been inaccurately characterized. Both Sherman and Prentiss reacted similarly to the warnings of the Confederate buildup, discounting the alarms until the fighting actually started.

But similarities in the experiences of their divisions end when contrasting how well and how long they were able to resist the Confederate attacks. The stand in Prentiss's camps was short-lived when compared with the stand of Sherman—mainly due to the terrain. The terrain on Prentiss's front offered his division few of the advantages that Sherman enjoyed.

Just as the Confederates during the battle encountered high water where the Corinth Road crossed the two streams just south of Shiloh Church, so the citizens living in the area prior to the battle found that same area difficult to traverse during the rainy season. Their solution was to construct a detour, called the Eastern Corinth Road, following a ridge passing between the headwaters of both Shiloh Branch and Locust Grove Branch.

Prentiss's division was bivouacked astride the Eastern Corinth Road, where the terrain offered fewer obstacles to slow the Confederates, thus providing attackers a much easier approach to Prentiss's camps than the Southerners attacking Sherman. A walk down the road to a point about 20 yards south of the Gladden monument will bring you to a red tablet for Gladden's brigade (stop 9A). Stand with the monument to your back to notice two blue tablets to the left. These mark a Union position on the south edge of Spain's Field. The Union force positioned itself at the

Braxton Bragg was apparently not aware that the attack led by Gladden was repulsed when he wrote that Gladden "fell early in the action, mortally wounded, while gallantly leading his command in a successful charge. No better soldier lived. No truer man or nobler patriot ever shed his blood in a just cause." (gam)

Along the way to the Hornets' Nest from Spain Field, a unique monument is located on the right or east side of the Eastern Corinth Road. When J. D. Putnam, Company F, 14th Wisconsin Volunteer Infantry, was killed, his comrades buried him and carved his name and unit into a tree. The stump of that tree has been duplicated as a distinctive monument on the battlefield where he fell in the famous Hornets' Nest on April 7. (gam)

J. D. Putnam is buried in one of the regimental plots alongside others with whom he shared his Civil War experiences. (gam)

ravine bordering the field and draining into Locust Grove Branch farther to the left. Gladden's men fell back to the ravine after the initial repulse of their frontal assault.

Walk back to the Gladden mortuary monument (stop 9B). Hit by an artillery shell during the initial attack, Gladden did not think his injury severe at first. "I am struck, but let's go on," he informed a staff officer. Soon the mounted general reassessed the extent of his wound. "It is a serious hurt, help me down," he beseeched of his aide. Gladden's arm was described as being "crushed into a mass of bones and flesh, near the shoulder." The arm was amputated on the field, but the doctors could not save his life. Gladden died on April 12.

From the Gladden monument, walking north toward Peabody Road for about 100 yards brings you to the cannon and blue tablet for Munch's Minnesota Battery on the left side of the road (stop 9C). Munch's 1st Minnesota Battery was the only Minnesota unit to fight in the battle of Shiloh. When the gunners heard shooting from their camp, they were ordered to the front, but were still uncertain what all the commotion was about. Before they could get off their first round, one of the gunners was shot. Private William Christie wrote, "The bullets were pouring upon us like a hail storm. Just as soon as we got our guns into position we began to give them our compliments with shell and canister. But we had not been there long when the regiments that were supporting us broke and fled."

The Union infantry may have moved hastily, but it did not actually break. The men withdrew from the edge of the ravine under Prentiss's orders. The Confederates, meanwhile, had regrouped after Gladden's wounding and attacked again, striking at the same time the Union troops were withdrawing across the field.

Battery commander Capt. Emil Munch "was severely wounded in the thigh," wrote Christie. "His horse was killed" and one of his men helped him mount another horse. "We limbered-up and fell back a short distance; unlimbered again, and poured the canister into them," as the battery apparently conformed to Miller's new position on the north side of Spain Field.

Behind the Gladden monument, a trail runs through the woods about 40 yards and into the field to the black marker for "Spain Field" (stop 9D). From there, you can easily see the blue tablets to the right marking where Miller's brigade repulsed Gladden along the south end of the field, as well as the blue tablets to the left marking both Miller's initial as well as his final position along the north end of the field. The marker to your left, closest to the Eastern Corinth Road, indicates the position of Hickenlooper's 5th Ohio Battery.

During the first Confederate attack, Captain Hickenlooper and his battery were posted near the north side of the field. Hickenlooper recalled how the fight in the field erupted: "Soon the banshee-like scream of the hurtling shell, the crash of timber, the volleys of musketry and the cheers of the charging regiments, all blended in one mighty rumble and roar, told in no unmistakable terms that the battle of Shiloh was on."

➔ TO STOP 10

Drive back down the road 0.1 mile north, returning to the intersection with Peabody Road. Turn right and drive 0.9 mile. Park in the small pull-off on the right side of the road just past the tall Arkansas Monument.

At The Hornets' Nest

The Hornets' Nest is perhaps the most iconic and famous place on the Shiloh landscape. The name itself—originating from Confederate soldiers who thought the amount of lead and iron fired out from the Union stronghold whizzing around them was reminiscent of a swarm of angry hornets—offers imagery to which most people can relate.

The Minnesota monument, across from the pull-off, marks the subsequent position of Munch's Battery after it fell back from its position covered during the last stop. If you face the same direction as the soldier on the monument, with the monument behind you, you'll be standing in the Sunken Road in the prominent Hornets' Nest area.

Later in this tour, we will follow a walking tour along the Sunken Road, which will return to the Hornets' Nest to provide you with ample opportunity to explore this heavily monumented area.

➔ TO STOP 11

Continue driving along the Eastern Corinth Road for 0.3 mile. Turn right on the Corinth Road and travel 0.3 mile. Turn left on the Hamburg-Savannah Road, which after 0.1 mile makes a 90-degree bend and becomes what is identified as either Jones Field Road or Cavalry Road. Continue 0.8 mile past the bend in the road to a pull-off on the right in the middle of a large field. Along the way, skip the pull-off for a park tour stop at a Confederate Burial Trench—we will visit it later.

CHAPTER SEVEN

April 6, 1862—mid-morning to early afternoon

When Prentiss retreated, he did not encounter reinforcements until he reached the Sunken Road, a mile to the rear of his camps. Sherman, however, had the benefit of McClernand's division camped just behind him, with one of the brigades taking position in rear of Sherman's first line at Shiloh Meeting House. Then when Sherman's forces gave way, the rest of McClernand's division joined Sherman in a position a mere quarter-mile behind his first stand at what has come to be known as the "Crossroads" position—the intersection of the Hamburg-Purdy Road with the Corinth Road.

Sherman gathered the remnants of his division to the right of McClernand along the Hamburg-Purdy Road. Lieutenant Patrick White of Barrett's Battery declared that Sherman was "the coolest man I saw that day." Even though he had multiple horses shot from under him—with a staff officer helping Sherman catch a stray horse near the Crossroads after one of his mounts went down—once the fighting began, nothing seemed to bother the otherwise nervous general.

While Sherman seemed to be able to make sense out of the chaos, confusion otherwise reigned conspicuously in this phase of the battle. A Union soldier slightly wounded in the leg and sent to the rear by his captain limped back to the front, rejoining the ranks and informing the officer who sent him away, "Cap, give me a gun, this blamed fight ain't got any rear."

One of Sherman's officers recalled the scene as the remnants of the division formed up west of the Crossroads:

Here was more confusion than I saw at any time during the day. The troops who retained their organization were

The straight row of four Illinois regimental monuments just beyond this artillery unit clearly mark the battle line of Raith's and Marsh's brigades. (gam)

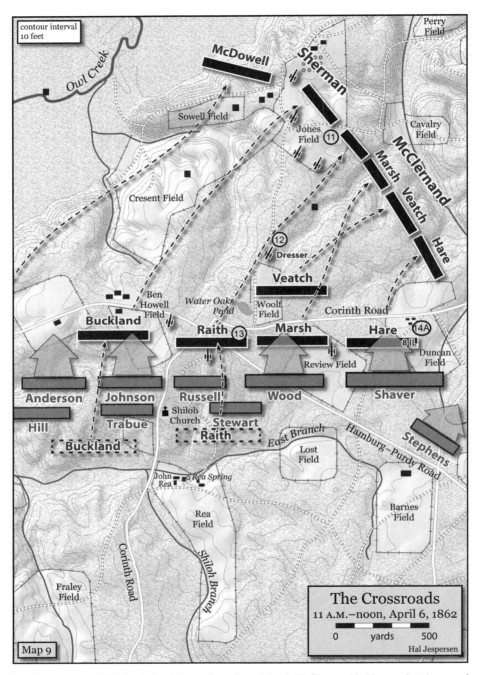

THE CROSSROADS—With the help of troops from Gen. John A. McClernand in bivouac just in rear of Sherman, soldiers from the Union Shiloh Church position rallied at the Crossroads of the Corinth Road with the Hamburg–Purdy Road. Outflanked by Confederates who had earlier driven Prentiss from his camps, the Union Crossroads position was only a brief stand.

in good shape, but there were many disorganized men; the road was almost blocked with teams [of horses] hurrying from the battle line; a battery was trying to get into position; the Confederates charged; there was a brisk fire for a few moments. Our line gave way at all points. As the line began to waiver one of our men called to me, 'See that cannon.' There was a brass gun stuck between two small trees, apparently abandoned by all but one man, who sat on the wheel horse crying.

* * *

When Prentiss gave way, Johnston quickly took two of the Confederate brigades that had already driven Prentiss from his camps—those of Wood and Shaver—and redirected them to attack the Sherman-McClernand line at the Crossroads. They were joined by a fresh brigade from Polk's third wave under Brig Gen. A. P. Stewart. This force of some 8,000 men had the strength and position to strike a crippling blow to the Union line. The attack on the left flank of this Union line, near Duncan Field, was primarily responsible for unraveling the entire position.

The 49-year-old John McClernand had a life that much resembled Abraham Lincoln's: he was born in Kentucky, was a self-taught lawyer, served briefly as a soldier in the Black Hawk War, and had been a congressman. But unlike Lincoln, McClernand was an anti-abolitionist Democrat from the pro-slavery region of southern Illinois representing a faction that Lincoln wanted to retain with the Union cause—so, for political purposes, Lincoln appointed McClernand to be a general. (loc)

Even though the Confederate assault was successful, confusion was prominent in their ranks as well. Fraught with multiple incidents of the Confederates accidentally firing into one another, the attack force became bogged down. General S. A. M. Wood rode toward one of the errant units to get it to cease firing into fellow Confederates when they shot at him, wounding his horse. The mount bucked, and although Wood was jostled out of the saddle, his foot remained stuck in the stirrup. The frightened animal dragged Wood along the ground, stunning the general and incapacitating him for several hours. A soldier in the 5th Tennessee observed a color-bearer step out in front of the battle line waving his flag, which fortunately "was recognized as a Confederate one and the firing ceased." Understandably, the attack sputtered to a standstill about 10:00 a.m.

* * *

In this short but brutal fight, Johnston drove Sherman and McClernand north from the Crossroads; they hastily reformed their men into a defensive line on the southern end of what is now called "Jones Field."

About 10:00 a.m., Grant consulted with Sherman, possibly in Jones Field. Grant's message to all he encountered that day was short and nearly identical: ammunition was heading toward the front, and the troops should hold on because reinforcements were also on their way—the troops

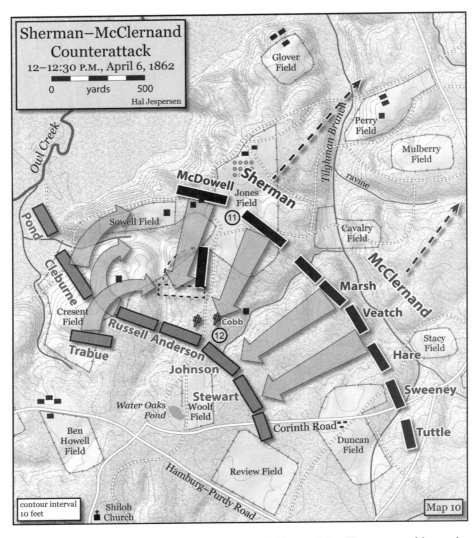

Sherman–McClernand Counterattack
12–12:30 P.M., April 6, 1862

0   yards   500

Hal Jespersen

Glover Field

Perry Field

Mulberry Field

Owl Creek

Tilghman Branch

ravine

McDowell

Sherman

Jones Field

Pond

Sowell Field

Cleburne

Cavalry Field

McClernand

Cresent Field

Russell

Anderson

Marsh

Veatch

Trabue

Johnson

Stacy Field

Hare

Stewart

Water Oaks Pond

Woolf Field

Cobb

Sweeney

Ben Howell Field

Corinth Road

Duncan Field

Tuttle

Hamburg–Purdy Road

Review Field

contour interval 10 feet

Shiloh Church

Map 10

SHERMAN-MCCLERNAND COUNTERATTACK—Confederate plundering in the camps of Sherman and McClernand and modest Union reinforcements enabled the troops who had fought at Shiloh Church and the Crossroads to regroup in Jones Field. They launched the most substantive Union counterattack of the day at about noon, but were eventually driven back to Jones Field.

of Lew Wallace's division and Buell's army would soon be up, he believed.

In this field, the promised arrival of some fresh troops emboldened Sherman and McClernand. Their efforts to prepare a defensive position here soon transitioned into a plan for organizing a counterattack—a bold move for a body of troops that had just been driven from its camps.

The audacious decision was made possible because the Confederates permitted the Union soldiers the time to reform. Just as Confederates had looted Prentiss's camps on the Confederate right, so hungry and irregularly equipped soldiers on the Confederate left could not resist the temptation of going through the captured camps of Sherman and McClernand in search of food and better weapons.

Beauregard soon recognized the problem; he directed his staff and his own cavalry escort to get the troops out of the camps and back into the battle. They eventually formed a line on the north edge of the area now known as "Woolf Field," about one-half mile south of the patchwork line Sherman and McClernand had assembled in Jones Field.

While the Union infantry planned their counterattack and the Confederate infantry was being persuaded to stop pillaging the camps, the artillery of both sides engaged in a spirited duel. With fifteen Union artillery pieces posted on the south end of Jones Field and Confederate guns positioned on the north end of Woolf Field, gunners in both armies could find targets through the intervening open woods. Soon all or part of three Confederate batteries—including Capt. Robert Cobb's Kentucky Battery—were joined by elements of five brigades in the thin woods just north of Woolf Field.

* * *

Though the Union forces had been roughly handled throughout the morning of April 6, those midwestern boys still had a lot of fight in them. Sometime between noon and 12:30 p.m., the battered Union troops of Sherman and McClernand had regrouped, been reinforced, and begun moving out of Jones Field to make what would be the most substantive attack of any Union force on the first day of the battle of Shiloh.

The right end of Col. C. Carroll Marsh's largely intact brigade of McClernand's division approached Cobb's position. Once Union troops passed over a slight ridge in front of the Confederate line, the fighting became intense and raged on for nearly another hour.

Federals shoved the Confederates back nearly half a mile, and the counterattack came close to reaching the Crossroads once again.

But the Confederates would turn the tide back in their favor. The last reserve brigade available to Beauregard—Col. Robert P. Trabue's Kentucky and Alabama brigade—arrived just in time. Trabue encountered General Hardee and asked what to do with his command. "Put it where the fight is the thickest, sir," was Hardee's imprecise order.

After the capture of Cobb's Confederate battery (above), Union Gen. McClernand momentarily regained his headquarters camp and could not help but notice how this familiar scene had dramatically changed. "Within a radius of 200 yards of my headquarters," McClernand observed, "the ground was almost literally covered with dead bodies, chiefly of the enemy." McClernand's headquarters is marked by a stack of cannonballs about 270 yards southeast of Cobb's Battery. (gam)

As Trabue assessed where the fighting was most intense, "I gave the order fix bayonets and move forward in double-quick time at a charge." Trabue ended up smashing into the Sherman-McClernand line at its most vulnerable spot—its right flank. The blow started to unravel the entire Union line that had advanced from Jones Field, and eventually all of the Union survivors fell back, again, to regroup, again, in that same field.

But the Union troops did not stay long in Jones Field this time. They repositioned farther east to a new position behind the daunting Tilghman Branch, once again presenting the Confederates with a substantial terrain obstacle to overcome before reaching the Union line.

At Jones Field

Walk to the orientation station on the left side of the road. The Shiloh Church area is just a little more than one mile in front of you, to the south. The wood line visible ahead marks the south edge of Jones Field. Sherman and McClernand organized their defensive line along that edge of the field.

The Crossroad—the intersection of the Hamburg-Purdy Road with the Corinth Road—is three-quarters of a mile ahead.

We will return to this stop again later in the tour to discuss the fighting that initiated the second day of the battle on the north end of Jones Field, behind you.

⟶ TO STOP 12

Continue driving down the road. In just 0.1 mile, the road will take a 90-degree bend to the left at the beginning of Sherman Road. Continue 0.4 mile to the point where the road widens at a pull-off; here is an orientation station on the right side of the road, and two pair of cannon facing opposite directions are located on the left.

At the Edge of Woolf Field

Walk first to the cannon with the blue tablet for Dresser's Battery, pointing south, the same direction you have been driving. The open area about 100 yards in front of you is the north edge of Woolf Field, and the Crossroads is about one-quarter mile farther.

After Sherman's division made its determined stand at the meeting house, it was forced back to the Crossroads for a second stand, this time with most of McClernand's division joining in a struggle of much less duration than the fighting at the church. As the Union forces withdrew from the Crossroads to Jones Field, Dresser's Battery D of the 2nd Illinois of McClernand's division sought to slow down the Confederate pursuit by dropping trail in the thin woods north of Woolf Field.

Sherman's artillery chief, Maj. Ezra Taylor, offered an exceedingly high compliment when he declared that the battery was "under the most terrific fire, perhaps, that occurred at any point or at any time during the fight." Taylor observed that Dresser's Battery "fought bravely till their horses were literally piled up, creating a barrier to the retreat of their guns," losing four cannon while covering the retreat.

With experience as a captain in the Mexican War, the 38-year-old Col. Robert Trabue took command of the brigade only a few days before the battle, replacing John Breckinridge when that general was elevated to take control of the Reserve Corps. Breckinridge recommended that Trabue be promoted to brigadier general because of his conduct at Shiloh, but before the rank was bestowed upon him he died of disease in February 1863. (hoob)

Turn around and walk back to the cannon, pointing north, and red tablet for Cobb's Battery. During the Federal counterattack here, at no place was the fighting more desperate than at Cobb's Battery. Union Col. C. Carroll Marsh's men shot down nearly all of the battery's horses and inflicted devastating casualties upon the Confederate gunners. Cobb indicated that only eight of the battery's 72 horses survived the battle and that 39 out of 84 men were killed or wounded. Marsh's men captured Cobb's six guns.

───▶ **To Stop 13**

Continue driving nearly 0.2 mile to the pull-off for Water Oaks Pond on your left. We will be returning to the Water Oaks area later in the tour to cover the April 7 action in this vicinity, but for now our focus will be on the April 6 action around the Crossroads.

At The Crossroads and Raith Mortuary Monument

From the pull-off for the tour stop, walk along the road shoulder ahead of you for one-eighth mile, carefully crossing the Corinth Road, stopping at the mortuary monument (upright cannon with four cannonball stacks) for Col. Julius Raith.

Stand so the Corinth Road is to your right and the Raith monument is to your left. The Corinth Road curves behind you and continues to Pittsburg Landing two-and-one-quarter miles away. Ahead of you the Corinth Road leads to the Shiloh Meeting House site, just one-quarter mile away, and you should be able to see the Shiloh Church Cemetery while looking down the road corridor from this location. The road in front, stretching to the right and left, is the Hamburg-Purdy Road. The intersection of the

Julius Raith (pronounced "rite") fell from his horse, shot in the thigh. His men began to carry him to the rear, but at Raith's insistence left him in a ravine near a stream and propped him up against a tree. His leg was amputated en route to a recovery hospital in Mound City, Illinois, but he died of tetanus. (gam)

Corinth Road with the Hamburg-Purdy Road is known as the "Crossroads."

Raith's first position was nearer to the church in the woods ahead of you, but his second position was here. To your left front are two small Illinois markers, with three more to your left rear—all in a straight row. Two of these five markers denote regiments in Raith's second position. Raith comprised the right portion of McClernand's line, which continued to your left rear for one-half mile to the edge of Duncan Field. Sherman patched together his tattered division along the Hamburg-Purdy Road to your right.

Sherman's men had held on for nearly three hours during their stand at the church, battered there by superior numbers of Confederates. Fortunately for Sherman, help was a mere quarter-mile behind his line—help from McClernand's division. The senior colonel of the nearest brigade was absent on leave because his wife had died, and the next officer in line was sick, so the third-ranking officer, Col. Julius Raith, learned on the morning of the battle that he would command not just his own regiment but a brigade of four regiments.

A widower with children ages 7 and 10, Raith was running a flour mill in Illinois before entering the Union army. Still, he had some experience as an officer in the Mexican War. He ordered his men into line of battle and moved to Sherman's assistance by 8:00 a.m. Raith took up a position behind Waterhouse's Battery just east of the church, too far to the rear to prevent Sherman's line from being flanked by the Confederates. Raith was, however, well positioned to impede the progress of the Confederate pursuit of Sherman's retreating men.

While Raith struggled to hold off the jubilant Confederates, McClernand formed up the remainder of his division along the portion of the Corinth Road just east

Raith fell mortally wounded only a few hundred yards from the Shiloh Methodist Meeting House at Shiloh, Tennessee. Ironically, he is buried in a Shiloh Cemetery, only a few hundred yards from the Shiloh Methodist Church (organized in 1807) in Shiloh, Illinois. (gam)

The Illinois monument honors the 3,957 casualties from the state who fell at Shiloh, including division commander W.H.L. Wallace, and brigade commander Julius Raith, who fell a short distance from the monument. Soldiers from Illinois served in five divisions and commanded four of the six divisions in the Army of the Tennessee at Shiloh. The statue of the mother of Illinois holds a sheathed sword in her right hand and supports a book of the history of Illinois—including the role her sons played in preserving the Union—with her left hand. Sculptor Richard W. Bock used his wife Martha as the model for the mother of Illinois. (cm)

of that road's intersection with the Hamburg-Purdy Road. McClernand also ordered Raith to withdraw and form on the right of his division line, just east of the Crossroads.

Raith's own regiment, the 43rd Illinois, was one of the last to abandon the Crossroads position, after their leader was hit in the thigh. Four of his men started to carry off the colonel. But before going far, he screamed in pain and asked to be left behind—Raith reasoned that the men would be of greater service fighting the Confederates than helping him to the rear. After he suffered on the battlefield all night, Union troops picked him up and tendered him medical attention, including the amputation of his leg. But he did not survive, dying April 11.

Return to your vehicle. At this point our tour will detour from the park's self-guided driving tour; we will continue our coverage of the fighting on the western side and center of the battlefield on the first day of the battle.

→ **TO STOP 14**

Drive 0.1 mile and turn left on Corinth Road. Drive 0.6 mile and carefully park in the pull-off on the left side of the road for Ruggles's Battery.

The Battle for the Hornet's Nest

CHAPTER EIGHT

April 6, 1862—mid-morning to late afternoon

The right wing of the Union army (under Sherman and McClernand) loosely linked with the Union center (under W. H. L. Wallace and Prentiss) in Duncan Field. They formed the second Union position of the day, centered on the Sunken Road, the scene of fighting from about 10:00 a.m. to 6:00 p.m.

From the Crossroads, where Raith's brigade held the right end of McClernand's position, the division line extended eastward, generally parallel to and south of the Corinth Road. The 8th Illinois of Col. Abraham W. Hare's brigade held the left end of McClernand's line posted on the western side of Duncan Field (see Map 9 on page 72).

Wallace's division approached Duncan's cotton field from the east. One of his brigade commanders, Col. James M. Tuttle, was joined by Wallace's division artillery chief, Maj. J. S. Cavender, and together they examined the field and the woods to the southwest.

Tuttle indicated that "Maj. Cavender and I rode forward to reconnoiter, and at that moment we saw a line of bayonets glinting in the morning sun. Owing to the formation of the ground, we could scarcely see the men coming, or tell if they were friends or foes. In a few minutes, the appearance of a group of rebel officers in the woods relieved us of all doubt."

"We are in for it now," Tuttle remarked. "I will form my line of battle. Bring up your guns and you can get a raking fire across the field."

Tuttle formed his men at right angles to McClernand, facing west along an "old washed out road," the Sunken Road introduced previously. Cavender's cannon went into battery on a thinly wooded ridge to the rear of the Sunken Road.

The glistening bayonets spotted by Tuttle and

Though Daniel Ruggles reported that he assembled 62 cannon in what became known as Ruggles's Battery, the eleven artillery units comprising this impressive line of guns were unable to amass all of their pieces, so 53 cannon is probably a more accurate figure. "The order was that when the piece on the left advanced and fired," explained Capt. Francis Shoup, "all were to come into action." (cm)

Daniel Ruggles, a 52-year-old, long-bearded, Massachusetts native whose marriage to a Virginia woman would also eventually wed him to the Confederacy, claimed that he accumulated 62 cannon on this line. (loc)

A 28-year-old West Point graduate, Francis Shoup was a native of Indiana, but apparently through his army service in Florida and South Carolina he bonded with the Southern culture and joined the Confederacy. After playing a key role—if not the predominant role—in organizing Ruggles's Battery, Beauregard appointed Shoup the army's chief of artillery after Shiloh. (adah)

Cavender were most likely from the Confederate brigade of Col. Robert G. Shaver. This brigade, including the future explorer Henry Stanley, earlier in the morning had driven Peabody's brigade from in front of and through its own camps. Shaver commanded one of several units that had been reoriented by army commander Johnston, swinging north from Peabody's bivouac to strike McClernand's troops in order to throw the blue-clad men into the Owl Creek swamps farther north.

About 10:30 a.m., Shaver advanced northward across the western edge of Duncan's farmland. His men targeted Hare's vulnerable left flank. While Shaver successfully shoved Hare further north and across the Corinth Road, Shaver suddenly realized that W. H. L. Wallace was well positioned to harass his right flank. In his report of the battle, Shaver recalled, "my right wing was very much exposed to the fire of their sharpshooters. To my extreme right the enemy appeared in considerable force."

Shaver called upon General Bragg for artillery support. "In reply, the enemy opened upon my command from a battery in front and one to the right," wrote Shaver, "subjecting me to a cross-fire." After Shaver stumbled upon the Union stronghold, his advance ground to a halt, but other Confederate efforts were soon trained directly toward this newly discovered position. The fight for the Hornets' Nest was about to begin.

*   *   *

The western edge of Duncan Field contains a feature that is nearly as famous as the Sunken Road and Hornets' Nest in Shiloh lore.

At about 3:00 p.m. on April 6, the Confederates began to mass what would become the largest concentration of artillery that had ever been assembled thus far on the North American continent. Of the estimated 115 cannon in the entire Confederate army, Brig. Gen. Daniel Ruggles accumulated a collection of some 53 cannon from units throughout the army. It became known as "Ruggles's Battery."

A unique situation provided Ruggles the opportunity to break the normal chain of command and call upon far more artillery units than a division commander in Bragg's corps would ordinarily command. Army commander Johnston's plan of battle called for the advance to be made with three of his corps all lined up *side by side* with one corps in reserve (see Map 5 for Johnston's Battle Plan on page 22). Second in command Beauregard, who was assigned to execute the plan, either misunderstood or decided to disregard his instructions from Johnston when he aligned the troops.

Instead, Beauregard stacked the corps up one *behind*

the other (see Map 6 for the actual morning fight on page 23). Shortly after the fighting got underway, the troops of the various corps became all intermingled and the problems with the Beauregard plan became so obvious that the corps commanders worked out their own solution. Starting about 10:30 a.m., each corps commander took control of a particular section of the battlefield, directing any unit in that sector whether or not it belonged to his corps.

Johnston controlled the Confederate right, Bragg the right center—including the sector opposite the Sunken Road and Hornets' Nest—Polk the left center, and Hardee the left. Bragg ordered repeated infantry attacks against the Hornets' Nest, including several failed attacks made by two of Ruggles's brigades. When word arrived of Johnston's death, Bragg took over direction of the Confederate right and turned the right-center over to Ruggles.

The new sector commander quickly decided to forego the futile infantry assaults and instead pound the Hornets' Nest with massed artillery. Ruggles's unorthodox authority to call upon any nearby units ostensibly gave him the ability to bring a large number of batteries to assemble along the west edge of Duncan Field.

Ruggles directed his staff to "bring forward all of the field guns they could collect" and to do so "as rapidly as possible." Hardee's chief of artillery, Capt. Francis A. Shoup, was instrumental here, demonstrating just what his branch of the army could do, and Shoup may have played

The cannon currently marking the position of Ruggles's Battery include a tremendous collection of many unique guns. Slight variations between the guns reflect the work of many different small foundries throughout the South that tried to manufacture ordnance at the outbreak of the war to try to meet the Confederacy's military needs. (gam)

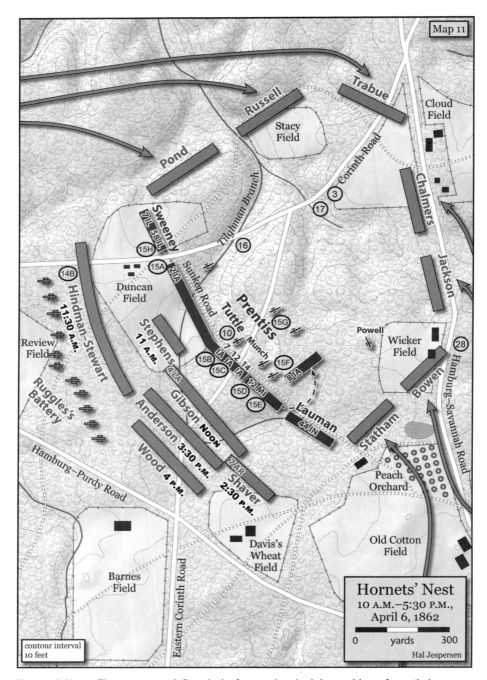

Map 11

Cloud Field

Trabue

Russell

Stacy Field

Pond

Corinth Road

3

17

Chalmers

Sweeney

7IL 58IL

15H

Tilghman Branch

16

Jackson

14B

15A

21IA

Duncan Field

Sunken Road

Prentiss

Tuttle

Hindman-Stewart

11:30 A.M.

Stephens

11 A.M.

4LA

10

7 · 12 · 14

Munch

15G

Powell

Wicker Field

28

Review Field

15B

15C

1IA 1A 1A 1A

15F

8IA

Hamburg–Savannah Road

Ruggles's Battery

15D

12MI

Bowen

Anderson

Gibson

NOON

3:30 P.M.

15E

Lauman

41IN

Statham

Hamburg–Purdy Road

Wood

4 P.M.

7AR

Shaver

2:30 P.M.

Peach Orchard

Davis's Wheat Field

Old Cotton Field

Barnes Field

Eastern Corinth Road

Hornets' Nest
10 A.M.–5:30 P.M.,
April 6, 1862

0   yards   300

Hal Jespersen

contour interval
10 feet

Hornets' Nest—The remnant of Prentiss's forces that had been driven from their camps encountered the fresh troops of Gen. W. H. L. Wallace and Gen. Stephen A. Hurlbut and went into position along a rutted wagon trace that came to be called the Sunken Road. Confederates named the area the Hornets' Nest and eventually surrounded the Union position, capturing 2,200 soldiers about 5:30 p.m.

an even more significant role in assembling the cannon than Ruggles.

Artillery is most effective when it is able to fire toward a bend or bulge in the opponent's position, where it is possible to fire down the length of a portion of the enemy line. Shoup recognized the Hornets' Nest as "the point from which the enemy's line bent back toward the landing." "I saw the opportunity for some more flank fire," Shoup observed, "and set to work to gather the fragments of our batteries, scattered about in all directions, and held them under cover of a skirt of woods on the further side of this little field." The "little field" Shoup mentioned is Duncan Field, and the "skirt of woods" is that on the western edge of the field.

Around 4:00 p.m. Ruggles's Battery opened in full force against the Hornets' Nest position. The primary target of Ruggles's Battery was apparently Cavender's artillery on the wooded ridge behind the Sunken Road. "The fire opened beautifully," reported Shoup, "but almost immediately the blue coats on the heights over against us began to break to the rear." Ruggles's Battery succeeded in driving away all of Cavender's artillery.

*   *   *

Between the time when the Confederates drove McClernand from his position south of the Corinth Road at about 10:30 a.m. and when Ruggles's Battery drove off Wallace's artillery at about 4:30 p.m., Confederate infantry launched a series of attacks against the Hornets' Nest.

The first assault was made by an understrength brigade of fewer than a thousand men, a brigade whose commander was unable to provide much leadership in the attack. Its senior officer, Col. William H. Stephens, wrote that he had "prematurely risen" from his sickbed and was then "thrown from my wounded horse," both of which "disabled me from rendering active assistance during the engagement."

Additional direction was provided, though, by Stephens's hard-fighting, hard-drinking, colorful-swearing division commander, Maj. Gen. Benjamin Franklin Cheatham. Cheatham first called upon a battery to soften the Union position and to knock out a Union battery to the rear of the Sunken Road before sending the infantry across the field.

At about 11:00 a.m., Cheatham reported that he "put the brigade in motion at double-quick time across the open field." Yet, as Cheatham further described, "So soon as the brigade entered the field the enemy opened upon us from his entire front a terrific fire of artillery and musketry, but failed altogether to check our movement until we reached

During the second day of the battle, the 4th Kentucky in the Confederate brigade under Col. Robert Trabue fought in north Duncan Field. Among the ranks of the regiment was George W. Johnson, the Confederate governor of Kentucky. Johnson began the battle as an aide, but when his horse was killed he decided to enlist as a private in the 4th Kentucky. In the fight, governor-private Johnson fell mortally wounded—shot in the thigh as well as the abdomen—and was left for dead upon the field. Union troops carried him away to a steamboat, where he died. (cwk)

the center of the field, when another part of the enemy's force, concealed and protected by the fence and thicket to our left, opened a murderous cross-fire upon our lines, which caused my command to halt and return their fire."

The 2nd Iowa monument sits along Duncan Field. During the first Confederate attack against the Sunken Road, the 7th Kentucky of Stephens's brigade began the attack moving across the open field, but later sought cover in the woods on the south side of Duncan Field. "We began the charge in good spirits," according to the regiment's Capt. W. J. Stubblefield, "but when we got well into the field the enemy infantry as well as artillery tuned loose on us with terrible effect and our Colonel commanded us out to the right of the timber." (gam)

The 2nd Iowa fired into the left flank of the attackers. Wallace's left and Prentiss's right (in the "thicket" Cheatham described: the Hornets' Nest) later joined in the fight, peppering the right of Stephens's line. The combined firepower repulsed this first attack on the Sunken Road and Hornets' Nest.

Stephens apparently reformed and attacked a second time, also unsuccessfully. The brigade would not make another attempt to strike this bastion of strength. They instead moved off to the right where they joined in the later, more fruitful efforts to flank the Hornets' Nest to the east.

But many more attempts from other commands to storm the Hornets' Nest were yet to come.

*   *   *

Ironically, the largest number of troops assembled by the Confederates for a planned attack against the Hornets' Nest never actually materialized. Shortly after the repulse of Stephens's brigade, some 3,700 Southern soldiers were massed on the far side of Duncan Field, from the Corinth Road to woods of the Hornet's Nest.

Shavers's brigade—which had earlier come under fire from troops in the Sunken Road—soon withdrew from the attack force because it was out of ammunition, and some other units followed suit. Apparently at this juncture, Brig. Gen. Thomas C. Hindman's "horse was killed under him by a cannon-ball and himself disabled by the concussion of the ball and the fall of his horse." Lacking overall leadership, some Confederates veered north and attacked Sherman and McClernand instead. Those Confederates who stepped out of the tree line into the field and in the direction of the Sunken Road, at about 11:30 a.m., soon pulled back to the cover of the woods after coming under fire.

About the time of this aborted assault, the Confederate corps commanders devised their informal method of dividing the battlefield into sectors, and Braxton Bragg arrived to supervise operations against the Hornets' Nest. Unfortunately, on the Shiloh battlefield, Bragg repeatedly displayed his lack of understanding for leading inexperienced troops and novice officers. Bragg often displayed outright contempt for his troops, and he was a marked contrast to the way Johnston provided encouragement for his men, achieving substantive service from the green forces under his control.

One characteristic of the fighting for the Hornets' Nest throughout the next several hours was Bragg's obstinate insistence on launching repeated assaults using nearly identical tactics from which he expected different results, and castigating those who suggested other alternatives.

Colonel Randall Gibson, commanding the Louisiana and Arkansas brigade, made the subsequent three or four attacks against the Hornets' Nest. The Confederate experience in the struggle to take the Hornets' Nest is best exemplified by these multiple attacks.

Bragg had been a neighbor of Gibson's before the war but had not gotten along with some members of Gibson's family. Then on the march to Shiloh, Bragg was embarrassed by Gibson when the young colonel asked General Johnston a question, and the army commander in turn sought an explanation from Bragg as to why one of his subordinates was ill informed. Those prior experiences may explain why Bragg was so severe with the officers of this brigade during the afternoon of April 6.

At about 2:00 p.m., the brigade made its first attack on the Hornets' Nest. "At the command to advance we charged up the hill into an almost impenetrable thicket," reported Col. Henry Allen, commanding Gibson's 4th Louisiana. "The enemy opened a deadly fire, which was quickly returned," as Gibson's first attack was repulsed.

Gibson concluded that the Confederates also needed artillery to counter the damaging Union guns. Since the battery assigned to accompany the brigade was left behind in Corinth as part of the city's garrison, Gibson lacked the ability to commit any cannon to the fight. If artillery support were to be used, it must come from a higher authority, and Bragg commanded that sector of the battlefield. But when the aide who had been sent to ask Bragg to send artillery returned, Gibson frustratingly learned that "[t]he request was not granted." Instead, Gibson indicated that the aide "brought me orders to advance again on the enemy." A second assault was made and turned back.

Rather than conclude that the Union position was too strong to carry, Bragg fumed. Believing Gibson's brigade failed due to lack of leadership, he sent his engineer, Capt. Samuel H. Lockett—the same officer who had earlier reported the true location of the Union left flank

Johnston thought very highly of the 45-year-old Braxton Bragg, appointing him to command the largest corps in the army (numbering 16,279), assigning him to also serve as chief of staff, and tasking him with obtaining firearms for the entire army. Despite being a decorated artilleryman during the Mexican War, Bragg scoffed at Gibson's proposal to use Confederate cannon in the Hornets' Nest. (loc)

Each of the four regiments of Randall Gibson's brigade met with repeated failure attacking the Hornets' Nest. Though the number of attacks is difficult to determine with certainty, Gibson claimed, "Four times the position was charged and four times the assault proved unavailing." (sll)

One of Gibson's four regiments to strike the Hornets' Nest was the 1st Arkansas under future general James W. Fagan. "Three different times did we go into that valley of death, and as often were forced back by overwhelming numbers," Col. Fagan reported. "That all was done that could possibly be done the heaps of killed and wounded left there give ample evidence." (loc)

to Johnston—to carry the colors of Allen's 4th Louisiana into yet another attack. After taking the flag from the color bearer, Lockett reported, "An officer came up to me with a bullet-hole in each cheek, the blood streaming from his mouth, and asked, 'What are you doing with my colors, sir?'" After Lockett explained his assignment, the officer protested, "'Let me have them,' he said. 'If any man but my color-bearer carries these colors, I am the man.'" That officer was none other than Colonel Allen.

Allen sent Lockett back to Bragg with an observation as well. Since Bragg would not provide the request for artillery support, Allen believed the Confederates should go around the Hornets' Nest. "He must attack this position in flank," Allen insisted, "we can never carry it alone from the front." Perhaps it was at this phase that Bragg himself confronted Allen. "Colonel Allen," Bragg insultingly demanded, "I want no faltering now." Allen immediately obeyed the reckless order, and once again the attack failed.

Colonel Joseph J. Woods, the commander of the 12th Iowa, confirmed the repeated assaults against his position. "Soon he made a bold attack on us, but met with a warm reception, and soon we repulsed him," reported Woods. "Again and again repeatedly did he attack us, trying vainly to drive us from our position. He failed to move us one inch from our position. On the contrary, we repulsed every attack of the enemy and drove him back in confusion."

*   *   *

Likely because of Bragg's distorted perception that Gibson's brigade repeatedly failed to take the Hornets' Nest due to the poor leadership of its commanding officers, he

sent another brigade in their footsteps. About 2:30 p.m., Shaver's brigade moved forward in its third major attack of the day. Resupplied with ammunition, the brigade of Arkansans moved out over ground already strewn with the casualties of Stephens's and Gibson's attacks.

"On the enemy's right was a battery of the presence of which (so completely was it concealed) I was not aware until it opened," Shaver confessed. "I pressed forward, the enemy remaining close and quiet" until Confederate troops reached about 50 or 60 yards from their line, "when a terrific and murderous fire was poured in upon me from their lines and battery. It was impossible to charge through the dense undergrowth, and I soon discovered my fire was having no effect upon the enemy, so I had nothing left me but to retire or have my men all shot down."

The commander of the 7th Arkansas was killed in the attack. The major of the regiment reported, "when within 30 yards of the enemy's cannons' mouth, Lieut. Col. John M. Dean, our brave commander, fell dead, shot by a Minie ball through the neck while gallantly leading us to the charge." Dean apparently fell a short distance in front of the position of the 14th Iowa, because its commander, Col. William T. Shaw "placed a pocket handkerchief over his face and crossed his hands over his breast and we left him."

*   *   *

Benjamin Prentiss, with 1,100 men, had a greater influence on the battle than the numbers of his tiny command would suggest. Prentiss's men fought with determination and played a role in repulsing each of the attacks against the Hornets' Nest.

The 19th Louisiana of Gibson's brigade probably confronted the guns of Capt. Andrew Hickenlooper. The regiment's Col. B. L. Hodge wrote: "Seeing that my men were being rapidly shot down, and having no reason to believe that we were inflicting equal injury upon the enemy, I gave the order to cease firing and to charge bayonets." When Hodge discovered his men caught in a terrible cross-fire, he ordered a withdrawal. Hickenlooper vividly described the struggle around his guns "The ear-piercing and peculiar 'rebel yell' of the men in gray and the answering cheers of the boys in blue rose and fell with the varying tide of battle; and with the hoarse and scarcely distinguishable orders of the officers, the screaming and bursting of shell, the swishing sound of canister, the roaring of volley-firing, the death screams of the stricken and struggling horses, and the cries and groans of the wounded, formed an indescribable impression." (bl)

The first park historian, David W. Reed, was a member of the 12th Iowa and was posted here during the battle. Human nature inherently affected his work, and he placed more importance on the impact the fighting in the Hornets' Nest had on the overall battle than modern historians now credit. However, Reed's emphasis helped make the Hornets' Nest a famous landmark. (gam)

Major James E. Powell of Prentiss's 25th Missouri—the officer who commanded the Union patrol that fired the opening Union shots in Fraley's Field—was among the soldiers from the morning fight to form up in the Sunken Road. While fighting beside Hickenlooper's Battery, Powell fell, mortally wounded, while repelling one of the Confederate attacks. Among the many family members accompanying soldiers on the Shiloh battlefield was Powell's son, said to be a drummer boy who was "the idol of the regiment" but now surrounded by one of the most horrifying scenes the world had ever witnessed—and without his father's support.

Late in the morning, shortly after Stephens's attack against the Sunken Road had been thrown back, "Maj. Gen. U. S. Grant appeared upon the field," and according to Prentiss, "I received my final orders, which were to maintain that position at all hazards."

Shortly after Grant's second visit with Prentiss at about 4:30 p.m., Hurlbut concluded that he could no longer resist the Confederate attacks on his eastern sector of the Sunken Road, and withdrew to Pittsburg Landing. The movement exposed Prentiss's left flank, and he might well have decided to conform to Hurlbut's movement and withdraw his own command, too, but he did not.

One of three colonels in Gibson's brigade at Shiloh destined to become generals, Henry Allen protested when Bragg sent his engineer to carry the colors of his 4th Louisiana regiment. "Tell General Bragg I will see that these colors are in the right place," Allen insisted. (lsu)

Although Grant had offered similar instructions to all of his division commanders on April 6, Prentiss seemed to interpret the orders to hold his position "at all hazards" differently from any of the other officers. "I was in constant communication with Generals Hurlbut and Wallace during the day," Prentiss reported, "and both of them were aware of the importance of holding our position until night." But Hurlbut's withdrawal made it clearly evident that he had made no such commitment to sustain the position centered on the Hornets' Nest until nightfall. Hurlbut vacating his

Munch's Minnesota Battery posted a section of two guns on each side of the Eastern Corinth Road—one where the monument with cannon stands today and another on the south side of the road where a blue marker and cannon are exhibited. William Christie, who served in the pair of guns posted to the south, wrote to his father, "After some hours of this work and the repulse of several attacks, the enemy evidently saw that our guns were few in number," and "they crept up through the heavy brush and timber, and suddenly poured upon us a terrible fire. . . . In the two gun detachment every man but one was hit." (gam)

portion of the line compelled Prentiss to make adjustments if he were to hang onto the Hornets' Nest any longer.

Prentiss later explained his reason to cling to the Hornets' Nest despite learning that Hurlbut had withdrawn from the Sunken Road: "When the gallant Hurlbut was forced to retire General Wallace and myself consulted," wrote Prentiss, "and agreed to hold our positions at all hazards, believing that we could thus save the army from destruction; we having been now informed for the first time that all others had fallen back to the vicinity of the river."

The key to appreciating Prentiss' subsequent actions is to grasp his conviction that the sacrifice of his command was needed to "save the army from destruction." Prentiss saw the need to buy time for the other three divisions— Hurlbut, who had been on the Union left, as well as Sherman and McClernand, who had been on the Union right—to establish a final position, one that would become known as "Grant's Last Line."

With Confederates advancing on Prentiss from the direction of Hurlbut's former position, Prentiss had to confront a new Confederate threat. Prentiss sent the artillery to the rear and repositioned his infantry. Portions of five regiments that had fought for hours in the Sunken Road, facing principally west, were pulled out of line and reoriented, facing predominantly south. Prentiss "refused his flank," in military parlance: the right flank of this line resting near the Sunken Road and the line bent back perpendicular to the road.

Prentiss also sent an aide to seek reenforcements. When none were forthcoming and Prentiss noticed that the Confederates had "passed between me and the river," he then "determined to assail the enemy . . . charging upon him with my entire force." Only then did Prentiss vacate the Hornets' Nest position, endeavoring to cut his way

Benjamin Prentiss might well have been remembered for blaming the onset of the battle of Shiloh on his subordinate, Everett Peabody, but he managed to spin his contributions in the Hornets' Nest fighting into being the key to the battle in buying enough time for the remainder of the army to establish Grant's Last Line. (loc)

out, while the Confederates were just as doggedly trying to prevent his escape.

*   *   *

Coinciding with the final Confederate infantry attack against the Hornets' Nest at 3:30 p.m., a pair of Confederate regiments also tested the Union line in the north end of Duncan Field. The Crescent Regiment from Louisiana and the 38th Tennessee from the brigade of Col. Preston Pond, Jr., advanced toward the Sunken Road.

Concealed behind cotton bales and the nearby Duncan farm buildings in the middle of the field—near the modern cannonball pyramid—were men of the 7th and 58th Illinois regiments, both in the brigade of Col. Thomas W. Sweeny, in W. H. L. Wallace's division. The Illinois soldiers fired into the vulnerable Confederate flank. About all the Confederates could accomplish was to drive the Illinoisans back to the east side of the field on line beside the rest of Wallace's men along the Sunken Road.

Just as the left flank of the Hornets' Nest was jeopardized by the withdrawal of Hurlbut, so the departure of Sherman and McClernand on the other flank was disconcerting to Sweeny holding Wallace's right. McClernand had withdrawn one-half mile behind Sweeny, and Wallace sent an aide to appeal for him to reestablish his link with the Union troops in Duncan Field but to no avail. Within an hour after repulsing the last Confederate assault on the Hornet's Nest, Sweeny was in peril. His 7th Illinois had extricated itself without difficulty, but the 58th Illinois was in danger of being cut off and scrambled to escape.

Wallace was informed that his right had collapsed. Soon he and the rest of his division were rearward, wondering if they could get away without the need to force their way through Confederates blocking their path.

*   *   *

When Ruggles assumed command of the stalled-out Hornets' Nest sector, he directed one more infantry attack, but then he decided to adopt a different tactic for dealing with the Hornets' Nest—shell it with artillery. The climactic period for Ruggles's Battery was a twenty-minute bombardment starting about 4:00 p.m.

Colonel Shaw of the 14th Iowa described the artillery salvo as a "tremendous barrage, the heaviest I ever heard." Wallace's outnumbered batteries were forced to vacate the ridge behind the Sunken Road, though the guns had

Among the common misconceptions of the battle for the Hornets' Nest include the appearance of the Sunken Road. Rather than being a deeply eroded, ready-made defensive position—as was the case with famous sunken roads on other Civil War battlefields—war-time descriptions indicate that Shiloh's "Sunken Road" actually contained only shallow wagon wheel ruts. (loc)

also been ordered to withdraw when Prentiss learned that Hurlbut had vacated the Union left.

The concerted efforts of Ruggles's Battery and the Confederate infantry enveloping both Union flanks ended the nearly six-hour Union resistance at the Hornets' Nest. But before it fell, about 10,000 Confederates had made as many as eight infantry attacks against the Hornets' Nest, losing about 2,400 soldiers, or 24% of their men, in the effort.

On the Western Side of Duncan Field

Walk along the row of cannon and, after reaching the eleventh cannon, walk to your left in front of the cannon, stopping at the 8th Illinois monument (stop 14A). The 8th Illinois held the left end of McClernand's line posted on the western side of Duncan Field.

Place your back to the Corinth Road, so you face south. From here you can readily see the Iowa monuments along the Sunken Road on the other side of Duncan Field.

Looking across the field and across the ravine to your left front, the Sunken Road enters the wood line on the southeast corner of Duncan Field. That area was the portion of the Union position called the "Hornets' Nest," near where you stood at the Minnesota monument during an earlier stop.

Walk back along the row of eleven cannon, looking to your right in the direction of the Sunken Road as you walk (stop 14B). Notice how little you can see of the Sunken Road from the Confederate artillery line. What you can see, however, is the wooded ridge behind the Sunken Road, which was Cavender's Union artillery position and the primary target of the Confederate artillery posted here. When Ruggles successfully drove away all of Cavender's artillery, the Federal gunners were promptly added to Grant's third and last line of battle, taking positions between the siege artillery and Silversparre's horseless battery.

The cannon along this line represent a wonderful array of different types of guns—take the opportunity to explore and examine these cannon, looking at the markings found most often on the muzzles of the guns and on the trunnions (in the middle of the cannon where the barrel is attached to the cannon carriage). The markings will usually identify the foundry, location, and year the cannon was made, and many name foundries that produced only a few artillery pieces for the Confederacy.

➤ TO STOP 15

Drive 0.1 mile and carefully park on the left side of the road at the pull-off for Duncan Field. Here the tour includes a walk of just under a mile, the length of the Sunken Road and Hornets' Nest.

At the Sunken Road

The center of the Union line in the Hornets' Nest was the scene of intense fighting and was the final portion of the Union line to fall during the second phase of the battle. However, the flanks of the Hornets' Nest were actually pounded harder than the center, and their breakdown led to the collapse of the position. (gam)

Carefully walk across the street to the Sunken Road. Stop at the first monument—that of the 2nd Iowa—and look across Duncan Field (stop 15A).

The 2nd Iowa on the right of Tuttle's line suffered several wounded by the Confederate artillery. One inexperienced soldier failed to appreciate the inertia of a seemingly slow-moving projectile. John T. Bell described how the soldier "threw his foot forward to stop a piece of exploded shell. . . . he thought had spent its force and instantly his foot is mangled and crushed." Bell was also beside Capt. Bob Littler when "a shell bursts directly in our front and a jagged piece of iron tears his arm so nearly off that it hangs by a slender bit of flesh and muscle and he jumps to his feet, and crazy with the shock and pain, shouts, 'here, boys! here!' and drops to the ground insensible."

The site of the Arkansas monument was selected to mark where Lt. Col. John M. Dean of the 7th Arkansas was killed. The regiment's Maj. James T. Martin wrote: "He died as a brave man and soldier would wish, 'with his feet to the foe and his face toward heaven.'" (gam)

Walk down the Sunken Road to the 7th Iowa monument (stop 15B). As Col. Randall Gibson's Louisiana and Arkansas brigade made its repeated attacks against the Hornets' Nest, the left end of Gibson's line probably extended to the north far enough to come under fire of the 7th Iowa.

Continue walking down the Sunken Road to the 12th Iowa monument (stop 15C). The left end of Gibson's line was the 4th Louisiana, led by Col. Henry W. Allen, which likely confronted the 12th Iowa. Allen noted, "While in this position a murderous fire of grape and canister was poured into us from the masked batteries."

Continue down the Sunken Road, cross to the south side of the Eastern Corinth Road and keep following the Sunken Road to a blue tablet for a section of Munch's Minnesota Battery. Then turn right and follow the short trail to the tall Arkansas monument (stop 15D). Brigade commander Robert Shaver spoke at the dedication of the monument and is said to have selected the spot where Col. John M. Dean was killed as the monument's location.

Turn left on the gravel road beside the Arkansas monument, walking away from the Eastern Corinth Road. When you return to the Sunken Road, veer right down

The location of state memorials usually indicate areas where troops from that state performed significant deeds. Two of the three regiments from Wisconsin fought in the Hornets' Nest, near the eventual location of the Wisconsin monument. The 18th Wisconsin fought in the vicinity with Prentiss until surrounded, with about 200 from the unit captured on April 6. Then on April 7, the 14th Wisconsin advanced through the area—John D. Putnam, whose grave was marked with the unique tree stump monument about 100 yards south, was a private in that unit. (gam)

the Sunken Road until you reach four blue tablets in a row, indicating the position of the remnant of Prentiss's division; the first tablet honors a portion of the 12th Michigan (stop 15E).

Turn around and now walk north along the Sunken Road, past the 8th Iowa monument to the gravel road. Turn right and walk down the gravel road in the rear of the Sunken Road position. Walk past the cannon next to the yellow tablet to a blue tablet for the 8th Iowa (stop 15F). When facing the 8th Iowa tablet, the next blue tablet to the left is for the 23rd Missouri of Prentiss's command. The units positioned here faced nominally south. Notice that the position marked by these two tablets is perpendicular to the Sunken Road position.

To meet Confederates advancing from the direction of Hurlbut's former position, Prentiss refused his flank to protect the end of his line. The loss of leaders in this refused flank position was staggering. Three of the colonels from these regiments were wounded defending this portion of the Hornets' Nest.

Walk back to the gravel road and turn right, continuing to follow the road in the same direction as before. Pass the impressive Wisconsin monument to where the gravel road reaches the paved Eastern Corinth Road.

Notice the cannon to your right (stop 15G). They represent artillery positions during both days of the battle, but during the April 6th fight for the Hornets' Nest, guns along this wooded ridge fired over the heads of the infantry along the portion of the Sunken Road facing across Duncan Field.

Turn left and walk down the Eastern Corinth Road (stay along the left shoulder so you face any oncoming traffic). You will cross a ravine immediately before you reach the Sunken Road—many Union soldiers utilized this depression for protection during the battle. Turn right at the Sunken Road and follow it all the way to the Corinth Road. Carefully cross Corinth Road and go to the small marker titled "Right of Tuttle's Brigade," near a lone, large tree in Duncan Field and stand with the road to your left, looking west across the field (stop 15H).

The monument to your right marks the position of the 58th Illinois and the nearly identical monument beyond it designates the location of the 7th Illinois. These regiments resisted Confederate attacks on the north end of Duncan Field.

 **To Stop 16**

Continue driving east along the Corinth Road for nearly 0.2 mile. Carefully park in the pull-off to the left, across the road from the W. H. L. Wallace mortuary monument.

CHAPTER NINE

April 6, 1862—late afternoon

About 5:00 p.m., W. H. L. Wallace received word that the woods beyond the right of his Sunken Road position were reportedly "full of rebels" (see Map 11 on page 84). The time to attempt a withdrawal had come. Wallace rode beside some of his men as they marched toward Pittsburg Landing through an open space. A Confederate skirmish line posted on a nearby ridge dominated the opening.

Suddenly Wallace "rose slightly in his saddle"—probably as a conscious effort to get a better view of some troops an aide pointed out to him, or perhaps lifted from the saddle by the bullet that had just struck him. Wallace "uttered a brief exclamation of pain," remembered his adjutant, Capt. William McMichael, "and then fell apparently lifeless to the ground."

"The ball entered above and behind the left ear," wrote his aide and brother-in-law, Lt. Cyrus E. Dickey, who was riding beside Wallace at the time, "and taking a slanting course passed out through his left eye." Everyone present thought that William H. L. Wallace was dead.

Dickey and three others tried to carry the body to the rear, but after about a quarter of a mile, the fighting was more intense than the skirmish fire where Wallace had been hit. "The firing became so hot on all sides that the men who were helping me let go," observed Dickey, "and I was compelled to leave him on the field."

* * *

Of the three division commanders who held the Hornets' Nest, Benjamin Prentiss was the last to abandon the belief that the position could be sustained. Prentiss held firm to the prospect that Lew Wallace's division would

Wallace's trust and confidence in Prentiss may have cost him his life. Wallace had been a lieutenant in the same company commanded by then-captain Prentiss during the Mexican War. Now serving side by side again at Shiloh, only this time as generals, the two acquaintances worked closely together. As in Mexico, Prentiss was the senior officer and Wallace once again followed Prentiss' lead to hold the Hornets' Nest until it was impossible to safely retreat.
(gam)

When Grant had his falling out with Halleck, the 54-year-old senior division commander, Gen. Charles F. Smith, commanded the army from March 4-17, and then resumed division command once again. Wallace rose to division command when Smith had badly skinned his leg stepping into or out of a small boat used to relay him from a steamer anchored in the river to shore and back. (loc)

arrive and deliver reinforcements, enabling the army to do much more than just hold onto the Hornets' Nest. Prentiss also naively expected to recover his camps, declaring that he would sleep in his own tent that night. Those prospects disappeared when Prentiss realized that Confederates were already closing in on his rear. Holding onto the Hornets' Nest was a forlorn hope.

Then, as Prentiss attempted to cut his way out, he realized he also had to abandon the goal of escaping when he reached Hell's Hollow. Troops primarily under Leonidas Polk blocked Prentiss's way in such numbers that Union soldiers could not expect to drive them out of their retreat path. As Prentiss reported, "finding that further resistance must result in the slaughter of every man in the command, I had to yield the fight. The enemy succeeded in capturing myself and 2,200 rank and file, many of them being wounded." Significant portions of six regiments—four from W. H. L. Wallace's division and two from Prentiss's own command—surrendered in or near Hell's Hollow.

The surrender was not instantaneous. Confusion reigned until everyone grasped just what had occurred. One Confederate officer suggested that his captives hide in tents of a nearby camp so other Confederate units yet to understand that a surrender had occurred would not shoot at the Union prisoners.

Some of the Confederates thought they had captured what remained of the Union army and that the battle was over. But soon the Confederates who had encircled the surrendered men were reoriented back into battle line and moved on toward Grant's Last Line. Most Confederates confronted but did not attack the final Union line that first day of the battle.

Beauregard further instructed his men to pull back out of range of Union gunboat artillery fire, now joining the fray. Beauregard concluded that if any of the battered Union army remained on the battlefield on April 7, the Confederate army could complete the victory on that day.

At the William H. L. Wallace Mortuary Monument

Ann Wallace, the general's wife and Cyrus Dickey's sister, had arrived that morning for a surprise visit with her husband. Ann, instead, spent her time aiding wounded soldiers aboard the steamer *Minnehaha* at Pittsburg Landing. Cyrus found Ann on the boat and shared with her what he believed to be true. "My husband was dead," Ann reported that Cyrus had told her, "and the enemy has possession of the ground where he lay."

But the following day at about 10:00 a.m., when Union

counterattacks recovered the place where Dickey had left the seemingly lifeless body of Wallace, he was discovered to be alive still. Laid near some ammunition boxes to protect him from being trampled upon, and now covered with a blanket placed over him by the Confederates, the heavy rain of the intervening night left the general "wet and cold" but breathing. The general was taken to the landing and placed on board the steamer right next to the *Minnehaha*.

Naturally Ann Wallace "flew" to her husband's side. "He knows me; he knows me!" she announced with surprise, later recalling, "Will recognized my voice and clasped my hand." Considering the severe head wound, others doubted that Wallace was capable of being so responsive.

Wallace was transported to the Cherry Mansion in Savannah; there, it is said, he was able to tell his wife, "We meet in heaven," before he died on April 10, 1862.

The 40-year-old William H. L. Wallace, a lawyer from Illinois, was a new general—promoted to brigadier general on March 21, 1862—who only took command of his division on April 4, just two days before the battle. (bl)

━━━▶ **TO STOP 17**

Continue driving east along the Corinth Road for nearly 0.2 mile to the Confederate monument on the right side of the road and park in the pull-off.

At Hell's Hollow—Prentiss's Surrender Site

The location of the Confederate monument on the knoll overlooking Hell's Hollow marks what may be considered the high-water mark of Confederate success in the battle of Shiloh. The capture was the largest number of Union prisoners taken by Confederate forces thus far in the war.

As you face the Confederate monument, walk down the hill to the right and locate the trail leading into the woods. Walk about 25 yards, going past the blue 58th Illinois tablet, and stop at the small blue marker stating that Prentiss "surrendered here."

As the shooting subsided, Union officers engaged in the military formality of offering their swords to Confederate officers. Prentiss turned his sidearms over to Col. William. H. Rankin of the 9th Mississippi—an officer destined to be mortally wounded within the next 24 hours. (gam)

━━━▶ **TO STOP 18**

Continue driving east on the Corinth Road for 0.25 mile. Turn left on the Hamburg-Savannah Road and drive 0.1 mile to a 90-degree bend to the left. Pull off on the gravel shoulder on the right, just past the black and white striped gate so as not to block the gate.

The Hamburg-Savannah Road

CHAPTER TEN

April 6, 1862—late afternoon

While W. H. L. Wallace, Prentiss, and Hurlbut fought in the Sunken Road, Sherman and McClernand largely fought their own independent struggle on the first day of the battle. Despite the lack of coordination between the two wings of the army, McClernand's troops inadvertently protected Wallace's right flank throughout most of the day.

After Sherman and McClernand fell back to Jones Field to regroup for the second time, they decided to continue their withdrawal and crossed over to the east side of Tilghman Branch in mid-afternoon (see Map 4 for Grant's Last Line on page 14). This put a substantial barrier between the opposing forces, and this barrier could serve the Union forces much as Shiloh Branch and East Branch had aided Sherman's defense at Shiloh Church. In doing so, the Union right wing also fell back to the Hamburg-Savannah Road, and very importantly protected the road by which reinforcements from Lew Wallace's division would arrive from their bivouac at Crump's Landing to the north. The movement also drew them closer to Pittsburg Landing, making it more difficult for the Confederates to achieve their objective of driving the Union army away from the landing and into the Owl Creek bottoms.

While the position taken up by the Union right wing had those three tremendous advantages, McClernand seemed unaware of the manner in which his new position contributed to the doom of the Union troops in the Sunken Road. The withdrawal of the Sherman and McClernand gave large numbers of the Confederate troops an opportunity to join in the fight against the Hornets' Nest and to flank W. H. L. Wallace's position.

Only two Confederate brigades and some Southern cavalry continued to retain contact with the Union right

Shortly after the battle ended, Union soldiers buried the Confederate dead in mass graves like this one. While only five burial trenches are identified today, of the eleven or twelve burial trenches the Union soldiers dug, all are on the western part of the battlefield. The trenches marked today are in Rea Field, near Shiloh Church, beside the Water Oaks Pond, just south of Jones Field, and here near the Hamburg-Savannah Road. (cm)

wing. About 4:00 p.m., Confederates took aim at the left of McClernand's new line, which he estimated to be his division's sixth position of the day. Battery D, 1st Illinois Artillery, commanded by Capt. Edward McAllister, supported that part of McClernand's line.

A Confederate brigade under Col. Preston Pond, Jr., targeted McAllister's guns. Pond wanted to know what he would be up against in the upcoming assault, so he went on a reconnaissance. Leaving his command in the Tilghman Branch valley, crawling along the edge of a ravine, through his field glass, Pond examined the Union position.

When he returned, he discovered that someone had concluded that his brigade was without a commander. Lieutenant Colonel Samuel Ferguson, a 27-year-old from Beauregard's staff, had been directed by General Hardee to take command of Pond's troops and attack the Union battery. Since Pond had just seen the enemy position with his own eyes, he directed Ferguson to "Go back and tell the General I fear he does not know the great strength of the enemy and the weakness of my command." Two of Pond's regiments already had been detached and were engaged with Sweeny in the north part of Duncan Field by this time. Nonetheless, when Ferguson returned, he reported that the attack orders stood.

Fortunately, Pond had discovered a fork of Tilghman Branch about an eighth of a mile north of the offending battery. The ravine of this fork concealed his brigade from enemy view as it neared the Union position. But rather than send all of his men out of the ravine at the same time to rush the guns, Pond made piecemeal attacks first with the 18th Louisiana, next with the Orleans Guards, then with the 16th Louisiana.

The men of the 18th Louisiana, under Col. Alfred Mouton, were at the head of the column, closest to the enemy. "Before we had gone 50 yards the battery opened upon us," reported Silas Grisamore of the 18th Louisiana. "Our company was next to the flag of our regiment, and the bullets rang out about our ears like bees swarming. Once only I looked behind me to see Col. Mouton's horse falling under him." In just a few minutes, the regiment lost 207 men—41 percent of their number. The Orleans Guard lost 90 men out of about 150. The 16th Louisiana, being last in the column, realized they could not succeed either. Pond's men wore blue state militia uniforms, drawing fire also from fellow Confederates, further compromising the brigade's efforts.

Although the attack failed miserably, what Pond's men had done was to serve as a diversion enabling other units from the Confederate left wing to turn the flank and rear of

A deluge pelted the exhausted soldiers who had fought all day as well as the Union reinforcements filing onto the battlefield. (bl)

W. H. L. Wallace and contribute to the capture of the men holding out in the Hornets' Nest.

Yet before the Hornets' Nest had fallen, the position later known as "Grant's Last Line," Grant's third of the day, had taken shape. Troops from the Hornets' Nest formed into position on the portion of this line situated behind Dill Branch; these tied in with the troops located behind Tilghman Branch and along the Hamburg-Savannah Road about quarter of a mile north of McAllister's Battery. Seeing this, at about 5:00 p.m., the part of McClernand's line that was dangling below the configuration of Grant's Last Line also withdrew into that Union stronghold.

By holding the Hamburg-Savannah Road, the Union army provided the opportunity for Lew Wallace's 5,800-man division to join the main army and play a key role in a second day of battle. After a huge communications glitch regarding which roads to take and just where on the battlefield Wallace was expected to go, resulting in a colossal delay in his arrival, his troops reached the battlefield on the evening of April 6. They formed to the right of Sherman, thus becoming the right flank of the entire army.

At the Hamburg-Savannah Road

Walk around the black and white striped gate. Of the three blue tablets along the road, stop at the middle tablet for McAllister's Battery and face it.

You are standing on the historic Hamburg-Savannah Road. The north end of Duncan Field is one-half mile to the left front. About one-half mile ahead of you is

The Union ability to hold the Hamburg-Savannah Road on April 6 permitted Lew Wallace's division to arrive and go into position in Perry Field, where it launched the initial advance of April 7. The Hamburg-Savannah Road is only 130 yards behind these cannon, Bouton's Battery I, 1st Illinois Light Artillery. This image is taken near the main park entrance. (gam)

Tilghman Branch, a stream with steep banks. A tributary perpendicular to Tilghman Branch is located about one-eighth of a mile to the right.

As Confederates took aim at the left of McClernand's line late in the afternoon, they were annoyed by the Union artillery fire on McClernand's left from Battery D, 1st Illinois Artillery, commanded by Capt. Edward McAllister. The battery held two different positions along McClernand's line behind Tilghman Branch—the first position about 300 yards in back of the branch and the second some 400 yards farther east along the Hamburg-Savannah Road (your present location). When Pond's Confederate brigade targeted McAllister's guns, they may have been in either of these two positions. The original park historian who wrote the tablets interprets the fighting as taking place when McAllister was positioned here, on the Hamburg-Savannah Road.

The closest elements of Lew Wallace's division went into position 0.6 mile to your right along the Hamburg-Savannah Road. See the appendix for more about the controversy of Wallace's march to Shiloh.

→ **To Stop 19**

Continue driving only about 100 yards to the next pull-off, where a Confederate burial trench will be on your left.

At the Confederate Burial Trench

An interpretive marker at the Confederate burial trench discusses "the cost of battle," but because of the number of unknown burials on the battlefield, the true cost of the battle may never be known. The burial trenches and the national cemetery give visitors the opportunity to reflect on these costs, known and unknown. (gam)

In the days immediately following the battle, Union soldiers buried the Confederate dead in as many as twelve burial trenches. By the time the park was established, only five of those burial trenches could be located and marked. This burial trench is one of the smallest on the battlefield.

The men assigned to the burial details were practical and the locations of the trenches are tangible evidence of locations of heavy fighting, locations where many dead were found after the fight. The location of this burial trench suggests that the Confederates lost a lot of troops near here. It could be that many of the soldiers buried here are from Pond's brigade and fell attacking McAllister's Battery.

→ TO STOP 20

As you proceed to the next tour stop, after about 0.4 mile you will cross Tilghman Branch. Be sure to observe the steep banks of the stream to appreciate what a substantial terrain feature they create and what an obstacle it was for the soldiers to cross.

From Tilghman Branch, proceed another 0.3 mile to the pull-off for Jones Field, which we visited earlier in the tour.

Fighting Resumes

CHAPTER ELEVEN

April 7, 1862—early morning to late afternoon

On the evening of April 6, General Beauregard decided to pull the Confederate army back from its advanced positions. Most soldiers withdrew to the captured Union camps to rest for the night, but not all Confederate units obtained such instructions. Pond's Louisiana brigade, accompanied by a battery and cavalry detachments, were somehow overlooked and had not received the orders to retire. Throughout the night they held a position in the northeast corner of Jones Field, far in advance of any other element of the Confederate army.

On the morning of April 7, Pond's troops confronted Lew Wallace's fresh division of 5,800 troops posted east of Tilghman Branch along the Hamburg-Savannah Road. Although Wallace's division greatly outnumbered Pond, it was also the only Union force upon the entire battlefield to be confronted by any substantial enemy force.

By 5:30 a.m., an hour-long artillery duel began. While the cannon blazed away, Grant arrived upon the field and ordered Wallace to attack.

With the coming of dawn, Wallace could see that he would need to cross one of the most formidable terrain features on the battlefield: Tilghman Branch. Wallace consumed nearly two hours crossing the deep ravine, then easily turned the left flank of Pond's small Confederate force. Wallace had accomplished this first step simply enough but then came to a stop.

Already under a shroud of criticism regarding the judgments he made during his march to the battlefield on April 6, Wallace since has also been censured for not aggressively attacking the disorganized Confederate left flank with his fresh troops on April 7. But his division was the only Union force west of Tilghman Branch. With

Dedicated in 2005, the Tennessee monument is one of the newest memorials in the park. (A full image appears on pp. xviii-xix.) One of the three figures stands ready to protect the battle flag as well as a fallen comrade. The color bearer kneels to help a wounded soldier, while the hurt soldier laying on the ground seemingly musters what strength he has to make sure the flag does not land on the ground, grasping the folds of the colors with one hand and the flagstaff with the other. (gam)

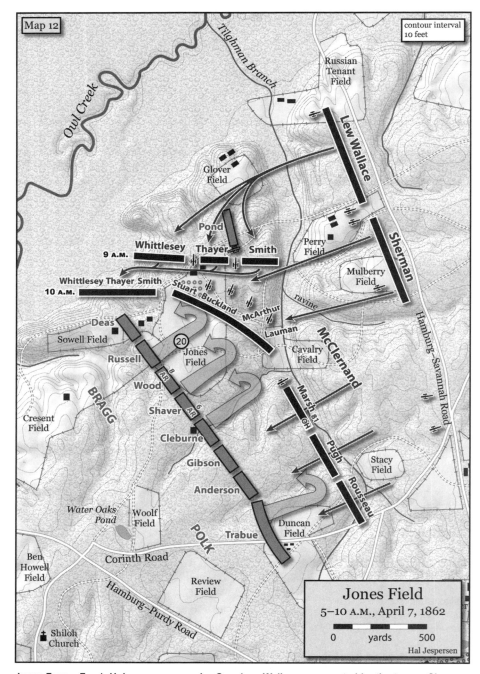

Jones Field

5–10 A.M., April 7, 1862

0   yards   500

Hal Jespersen

JONES FIELD—Fresh Union reserves under Gen. Lew Wallace, augmented by the troops Sherman could muster from the first day's fight, first engaged in an artillery duel and repulsed a determined Confederate attack, before launching a successful Union counterattack, driving Confederates back to the Crossroads and Water Oaks Pond.

Confederates appearing in force on the south side of Jones Field, Wallace did not want his lone division to become embroiled in battle with a substantial part of the enemy. Wallace was reluctant to venture further without support, so he waited for the other Union troops that were expected to join him.

That assistance was to come from other elements of the Army of the Tennessee—units battered on the previous day and, understandably, not in condition to move out as punctually as Wallace had done. So, Wallace halted across the north end of Jones Field, once again engaging the Confederates with his artillery, while awaiting troops from the remainder of Grant's army to move up on his left before advancing any further.

The morning attack of April 7 was not well coordinated. Sherman was listening for the sounds of Buell's army— the other reinforcements to join in the second day of the battle—to engage the enemy to the south before he felt he could advance to Wallace's support. At about 10:00 a.m., Sherman connected with Wallace, and the line advanced farther south.

Perhaps the role of no other general who fought at Shiloh has been scrutinized more than that of Union Gen. Lew Wallace. The 34-year-old Wallace has been criticized for his marching on April 6 as well as his fighting on April 7. Many who have studied the battle contend that Wallace has been unfairly maligned for both. (loc)

* * *

The tattered and tired Confederate army—an estimated 28,000 men that received only one regiment of reinforcements overnight—had regrouped. In this sector, Gen. Braxton Bragg patched together a line extending into the woods on both the south and the west sides of Jones Field.

Between the opposing battle lines, each side employed a thin line of skirmishers striving to determine the intentions of the enemy. Henry Stanley of the 6th Arkansas, selected for skirmish duty in the field, recalled that he was engaged within 20 paces of a "shallow hollow." Stanley wrote that he became engrossed in watching the Union skirmishers. In doing so, he failed to notice that he was suddenly too far in advance of the rest of the

Confederate skirmish line and thus was captured. Stanley became a "galvanized Yankee": after being held in a prison camp for two months, he chose to enlist in the Union army rather than wait to be exchanged and returned to the Confederate army. (In later years, Stanley showed more of this bold spirit by embarking on his career as a celebrated journalist and explorer.)

Upon Sherman's appearance in Jones Field, Wallace shifted to the west to flank the Confederate left, and both divisions advanced further south to this line. (gam)

Before the war, 39-year-old Sterling A. M. Wood practiced law and engaged in politics. At Shiloh, he managed to draw both praise and ridicule from superiors. Corps commander Hardee wrote of Wood: "though suffering from a fall from his horse, which compelled him to withdraw temporarily, returned to the field and bravely led his men." But his immediate superior, Hindman, filed charges against him—though a formal court of inquiry cleared Wood "from any imputation against him in connection with his conduct during the battle...." (wc)

The battle was renewed that morning with a vigor that surprised the troops in both armies. Confederates thought the Union army had been routed the previous day and anticipated easy fighting on April 7. Many boys in blue thought that when the Confederates had withdrawn on the evening of April 6 they had returned to Corinth.

Sometime that morning, the Confederates attacked. Beauregard witnessed the advance into Jones Field, "clapped his hands with joy, and declared that it was the grandest charge he had ever witnessed." The Confederate attack generally angled across the field from the southwest to northeast.

General S. A. M. Wood stepped off from the southwest corner of the field as part of the attack force. Union artillery waited until a majority of the Confederate battle line had advanced into the open before firing the big guns. Wood thought that the troops to his left would flank the Union artillery, expecting to see them "charge and take it." Wood reported, "I continued to advance, and had nearly crossed the open field to the woods beyond when the whole line to my left precipitately retired, falling back to the cover of the woods." The collapse of the Confederate left subjected the troops that remained in the field to "a destructive enfilading fire," according to Col. William. K. Patterson of the 8th Arkansas in Wood's brigade, and the survivors soon withdrew back to the south end of the field.

Other miscellaneous units of Grant's army joined in the battle, including the 81st Ohio previously under W. H. L. Wallace. It was probably in the woods near the southeast corner of the field that a soldier in the 81st Ohio observed an African-American: he had appeared on the front line, selected a position behind a tree near their position, and took shots at the Confederates with a "smile of intense satisfaction."

The fighting in Jones Field took on a back-and-forth character, until Lew Wallace achieved the greatest coup of the morning for the Union army. His accomplishment came not through brutal fighting, but by deft maneuvering. Wallace left his artillery in the field with Sherman while he shifted his infantry west of the field and completely outflanked the Confederates. Like spokes on a wheel, Wallace wheeled his line to the left and struck the extreme left flank of the Confederate army at about 11:00 a.m. "The whole Rebel Army broke and ran for their lives," an Indiana soldier in Wallace's division observed.

Beauregard responded by rallying his troops: he "rode up and made a short speech," according to a Tennessee soldier. Reinforcements rushed to the vulnerable Confederate left. Artillery fire became lively, and Beauregard ordered a counterattack that made no headway. The Confederates grudgingly gave ground, falling back. Eventually,

Confederate units ranging from the woods west of the field all the way to the Hornets' Nest were withdrawing, in an orderly manner, to the second Confederate position of April 7—the Hamburg-Purdy Road. Fighting resumed at this new line about noon.

*   *   *

Grant proclaimed that victory was assured on the second day of the battle when Wallace's division arrived upon the field. In making such a proclamation, Grant wanted to convince critics of his first-day performance that his own army could have successfully conducted the entire battle completely on its own.

But Grant did not have to rely exclusively upon Wallace for reinforcements. Major General Don Carlos Buell's Army of the Ohio had also arrived the same night as Wallace, adding another 13,000 to the ranks of the Union forces on the morning of April 7, as well as 5,000 more before the battle concluded. With Wallace and the remnants of Grant's army on the right, Buell's army comprised the Union center and left.

Brigadier General Alexander McCook commanded the division of Buell's army that linked with Grant's army north of the Corinth Road. McCook's men were first engaged on April 7 in Duncan Field, capturing five Confederate cannon before advancing further down the Corinth Road into Woolf Field.

After Wallace's presence on the Confederate left flank made the Jones Field position untenable, the second Confederate line of April 7 took form along the Hamburg-Purdy Road about noon. The Confederate defenders included numerous soldiers who had become separated from their commands and who now made up improvised detachments.

The fighting around Water Oaks Pond would perhaps be the most intense of the second day of the battle. Sherman described the fighting here as "the severest musketry fire I ever heard."

The opening exchange of gunfire in Woolf Field announced to McCook's men that they had stumbled upon a substantial Confederate position. A fresh brigade under Col. Edward N. Kirk passed through to the front lines, taking over the advance.

One of Kirk's men felt that the incidents of the previous twenty-four hours had readied them for what they were to experience. "I was quite well prepared for the occasion by hearing the cannons one whole day [April 6] and then passing through Savanna[h] where the wounded had been conveyed, but still more so by passing over the

A former teacher and successful lawyer, 44-year-old Edward Kirk was promoted to brigadier general in November, 1862. On December 31, 1862, he was mortally wounded in the hip in the only other battle in which he fought—Stones River, Tennessee—suffering for nearly seven months before succumbing on July 21, 1863. (bl)

A product of the Prussian military academy at Berlin and advocate of the theories of Karl Marx, the eccentric 51-year-old August Willich recruited a large number of Germans into Union service at the outbreak of the Civil War. (loc)

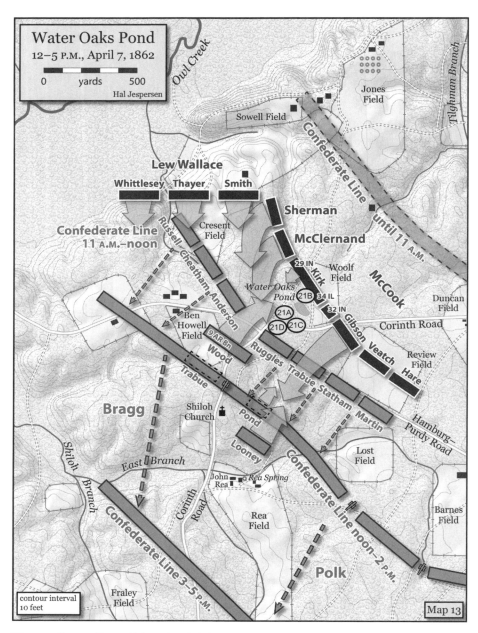

Water Oaks Pond
12–5 P.M., April 7, 1862

0   yards   500

Hal Jespersen

Owl Creek

Tilghman Branch

Jones Field

Sowell Field

Confederate Line until 11 A.M.

Lew Wallace

Whittlesey   Thayer   Smith

Sherman

Cresent Field

Russell Cheatham Anderson

Confederate Line 11 A.M.–noon

McClernand

29 IN   Woolf Field

Kirk

Water Oaks Pond   21B   34 IL

McCook

Duncan Field

21A

Ben Howell Field   21D   21C   32 IN

Gibson   Corinth Road

9 AR Bn   Veatch

Wood

Ruggles   Trabue   Statham   Martin   Hare

Review Field

Trabue

Bragg

Shiloh Church   Pond

Looney

Hamburg–Purdy Road

East Branch

John Rea   Rea Spring

Lost Field

Corinth Road

Shiloh Branch

Confederate Line noon–2 P.M.

Rea Field

Barnes Field

Confederate Line 3–5 P.M.

Polk

contour interval 10 feet

Fraley Field

Map 13

WATER OAKS POND—Union attacks in this area threatened the second Confederate position of the day. Confederate counterattacks buying time for a retreat to a third position and subsequent withdrawal from the battlefield, marked the last actions here.

battlefield where the dead, dying and wounded lay," wrote Bergun H. Brown of Kirk's 29th Indiana.

The attack of Kirk's 34th Illinois carried them directly through Water Oaks Pond. Here, though, Rutledge's Tennessee Battery beside the Crossroads poured deadly short-range canister artillery rounds into the attackers, while other cannon near Shiloh Church also joined in the fray. "The swish of canister and the droning of musket balls

Confederate General Benjamin F. Cheatham reported that the April 7 fighting near the Water Oaks Pond "was for four hours the most hotly contested I have ever witnessed." (sdm)

began to give us a new experience," recalled a member of the 34th Illinois. The soldier wryly calculated, "We began to realize that we were earning our thirteen dollars a month." Another Illinois soldier observed, "We had to cross a field about 40 rods wide and through a perfect storm of bullets, shot and shell. . . . Our men fell thick."

The commander of the regiment, Maj. Charles N. Levanway, was killed by a shell that hideously lacerated his neck. Kirk grabbed the regiment's battle flag and rallied the men, but he, too, was wounded in the fight, and the troops fell back to east side of Woolf Field.

McCook's final brigade to engage belonged to Col. William H. Gibson. Arriving in advance of the brigade was the 32nd Indiana. Its commander, Col. August Willich, was a Prussian-born avowed communist who had fled to the United States after fighting to overthrow the German monarchy in 1848. Willich's early war experiences earned solid reputations for both his regiment and him. At Shiloh, his confidence morphed into an arrogance that would shatter his command.

Initially held in reserve during Kirk's advance, Willich sought to go into action shortly after Kirk's repulse. "I asked General McCook for permission to pass with the regiment to the front and make a bayonet charge, which was granted," Willich reported. He ordered his command into a short but deep "double column" rather than in the more traditional long, thin line of battle.

Bayonet charges made in column formations in the Civil War were only successful when launched under just the right set of conditions, and the situation Willich faced at Shiloh wasn't one of them. Advancing to the left of Kirk's command, the compact column made an easy target. Willich's men were pounded by musket and artillery fire which "staggered it," according to McCook. Some of the regiment retreated

Similar to the way Johnston had been at the front on the first day of the battle, so Beauregard was in the thick of the fighting on the battle's second day when he then served as the army commander. (gam)

While many West Point cadets from the South resigned at the outbreak of the Civil War, the Alabamian Kelly resigned much earlier—in December, 1860—during the secession debates and in the aftermath of South Carolina becoming the first state to leave the Union. Appointed brigadier general on November 17, 1863, when 23 years old, he was the youngest general then in Confederate service. Rising to division command in the cavalry, Kelly was mortally wounded in a skirmish at Franklin, Tennessee, ten months after his promotion. (adah)

through the 34th Illinois, where Will Robinson described Willich's men as causing "almost a panic."

When the rest of Gibson's command arrived, McCook sent them into action south of the Corinth Road.

* * *

Though the Confederates held the Crossroads, they still had reason to be concerned about the stability of their position. Wallace's soldiers on the extreme Union right maneuvered around the Confederate left flank yet again, compelling the Confederates then to withdraw from their second position.

Beauregard established a third Confederate line for the day in the outlying Union camps, where the initial Union positions had been when the battle first began April 6. The troops that had been clinging to the Hamburg-Purdy Road at the Crossroads and Water Oaks Pond withdrew to the Shiloh Church ridge. In doing so, the Confederates had nearly abandoned all of the ground gained at such a high cost on April 6. McCook attacked again while the Confederates were withdrawing to the church cemetery, but the Southern soldiers soon struck back.

By this phase of the battle Wood's brigade had been reduced to a mere 650 men, but they still had plenty of fight left in them. About 1:00 p.m., his command (along with other detachments) advanced from the vicinity of Shiloh Church back to the ground they had earlier defended at the Water Oaks Pond.

"The charge was most gallantly made, crossing a pond of water in some places waist deep, and then entering an open field," Wood explained in his battle report. Major John H. Kelly, commanding the 9th Arkansas Battalion, "here displayed the greatest gallantry. He was on the right, and, dashing through the pond, sat on horseback in the open ground and rallied his men in line as they advanced. The enemy gave way and fell back in disorder, but soon rallied on our left so as to pour into us a cross-fire."

That crossfire came from Sherman's men, well situated on the north end of Woolf Field to assist McCook. Sherman's men unleashed volleys into the left flank of the counterattacking Confederates and drove them back toward Shiloh Meeting House.

Though Wood's attack successfully held the Union forces at bay, a member of Beauregard's staff questioned the ability of the depleted, exhausted, and demoralized Confederate line at the church to withstand another attack. Adjutant

General Thomas Jordan asked Beauregard, "General, do you not think our troops are very much in the condition of a lump of sugar thoroughly soaked with water, but yet preserving its original shape, though ready to dissolve? Would it not be judicious to get away with what we have?"

"I intend to withdraw in a few moments," Beauregard conceded.

About the time Beauregard decided to pull out, Gibson's Union brigade pressed forward east of the Corinth Road toward the Shiloh Church position. The Confederate army commander realized it would not be feasible to undertake a retreat while under attack. Yet another counterattack was necessary to relieve the pressure on the church line before he could hope to withdraw. Beauregard also recognized the need to personally lead that attack.

Beauregard grabbed the flag of the Orleans Guard Battalion to lead them to the left of the Confederate last stand in front of Shiloh Church. The general bellowed "Charge them, charge them my braves!" and attempted to lead them. A private near the general begged him not to be so conspicuous. "Never mind, my good fellow," Beauregard replied, "you do your duty and I will do mine." The private reasoned that while it was his duty to die, it was not one of the duties of the commanding general. Beauregard conceded and moved to a safer location. (bl)

Confederate brigade commander Col. Robert M. Russell observed that the subsequent charge was made "under the immediate eye of General Beauregard, who bore the colors in front of the line under the fire of the enemy." The general's staff as well as the soldiers in the ranks protested that Beauregard should not place himself directly in harm's way. But the general told his staff, "The order must now be 'follow,' not 'go'!" As Johnston had done on the first day of the battle, so Beauregard had recognized the need for the army commander to rally the men who had never before experienced anything so cataclysmic in their lives as the battle of Shiloh.

Pond's Louisianans, who had begun the day's fight in Jones Field, would be involved in the last of the Confederate attacks before the retreat commenced, including the attack led by Beauregard. Russell concluded that "courage and human endurance could stand no longer against such odds, and our forces were compelled to fall back to the hill where the church is situated. Our troops had now nearly all retired, and a final stand was made by a few regiments to cover the retreat."

The retreat began about 2:00 p.m. Breckinridge's corps, which had held the right center of the Confederate line on April 7, made up the rear guard. Unlike the other three Confederate positions taken up by the army throughout the day, there was no expectation that Breckinridge could hold his line indefinitely. His instructions were to hold off the Union army only long enough for the rest of the Confederate army to escape. "This retreat must not be a rout, sir," Beauregard counseled Breckinridge.

Some 5,000 of Breckinridge's troops took up a position south of Shiloh Branch. The stream could serve as a substantial barrier to the Union pursuit of April 7, just as it had been an obstruction to Confederate attacks on Sherman's position on April 6.

Yet another counterattack was needed to give Breckenridge time to set up the rearguard. Once more, fighting took place just south of the Crossroads. The task fell to about 1,000 men, from various commands under the direction of Col. Robert F. Looney of the 38th Tennessee from Pond's brigade, who attacked three times.

About 5:00 p.m., Breckinridge concluded that all other elements of the army had retreated from the battlefield, and so he did the same with his command as they continued to cover the rear of the army.

At Jones Field

Lew Wallace's troops held this line until Sherman arrived in Jones Field. (gam)

From the pull-off, walk further ahead down the road to the west. While doing so, look to your right to the far side of the field and stop when you see the white base of a pyramid of cannonballs; stand facing it. Two cannon and tablets near it mark one Union position. Depending on the time of year that you visit and the type of crops in the field, you might also be able to see another, closer Union battle line marked with three cannon and tablets. Between your location and the near Union line is a shallow ravine, which today has a thin line of trees growing in it.

Pond's position at dawn of April 7 is not visible from your location because it is hidden by trees, but it was in the corner of the field to your far right-front.

The two cannon and line of blue oval markers on the far side of the field near the pyramid of cannonballs mark where Wallace's men went into position on the north end of Jones Field about 9:00 a.m. The three cannon and line of blue oval tablets closest to you and closer to the ravine near the middle of the field mark where Sherman's infantry and batteries from various divisions of the Army of the Tennessee went into position about 10:00 a.m., beside Wallace's troops.

The center of Bragg's Confederate force was to your left and rear in the southwest corner of Jones Field.

The "shallow hollow" Henry Stanley mentioned in

his writing is very likely the same ravine ahead of you—
between you and the tablets for Sherman's battle line.

➤ TO STOP 21

*Continue driving down the road. In just 0.1 mile, the road will take a
90-degree bend to the left at the beginning of Sherman Road. Continue
0.6 mile to the pull-off for the Water Oaks Pond and the orientation
station (stop 21A), both on your left.*

At Water Oaks Pond

As you face the orientation station
marker and look down the road toward Jones
Field from which you just came, you are
facing northeast. The open ground beyond
Water Oaks Pond to your right is Woolf
Field. The first road to your right rear is
Corinth Road. Behind you is the Crossroads
intersection of the Corinth Road with the
Hamburg-Purdy Road.

Walk to your right front to the 34th Illinois
monument north of the pond (stop 21B). The
regiment advanced through this area, right
through the pond. Notice the cannon in the
Confederate line on the other side of the pond,
which wreaked havoc on the Union forces.

Also observe the obelisk monument
marking the position of the 32nd Indiana and
their ill-advised bayonet charge.

Walk back toward the orientation
station, passing it and the Tennessee monument. Continue
to the cannon and red oval tablet for Rutledge's Battery
(stop 21C); here at the Crossroads, Rutledge's Battery fired
upon the 34th Illinois and other blue-clad troops.

Turn about-face to walk toward another red oval tablet
beside Sherman Road for Wood's command (stop 21D), the
location of his desperate counterattack to buy precious time
for the Confederates. When you turn around to face the
Crossroads, you'll also see the Raith mortuary monument.

**Confederates tore down the
tents from the Union camps
in Woolf Field so troops like
the artillerymen of Rutledge's
Battery could more easily
target enemy forces. Union
losses in Woolf Field were
heavy. Of the eight brigades
of Buell's army to be intensely
engaged at Shiloh, only one
other brigade suffered more
casualties than Kirk's brigade
in its fight at Water Oaks
Pond. Kirk lost 346 men—13%
of his strength. (gam)**

➤ TO STOP 22

*Continue driving 0.25 mile and turn left onto Hamburg–Purdy Road.
After driving 0.8 mile, cross over the Eastern Corinth Road. Continue
another 0.2 mile and pull off to the right. Walk ahead to the orientation
station on the right side of the road (stop 22A).*

$\mathcal{F}$ields
of $\mathcal{W}$heat and $\mathcal{C}$otton

CHAPTER TWELVE

April 7, 1862—mid- to late morning

Breckinridge commanded the only Confederate corps to assemble all of its brigades side by side for the start of the second day of battle. Perhaps for that reason his corps was selected as the logical force for Beauregard to use to spearhead his attack of April 7. As Breckinridge's entire reserve corps moved out to the north, its soldiers expected to complete the Confederate victory that they felt they had nearly gained on April 6.

Colonel John D. Martin commanded the brigade on the right end of Breckinridge's line. Martin's men straddled the Eastern Corinth Road and stepped off across Davis's wheat field. "Our men cheered and rushed forward," Martin reported. But instead of finding the remnants of a defeated Union army, Breckinridge's men quickly encountered Buell's fresh reinforcements in a line of battle near the Hornets' Nest.

Martin indicated that his troops, "made three different charges upon the enemy, driving them back every time" until they were alarmed to discover "a large force of the enemy flanking us on the right." With this discovery, Martin "ordered the brigade to fall back" as Union forces pursued on its heels. "It was a wild pursuit, for a long distance, over rough country," remembered Lt. Charles H. Hills of the 41st Ohio. "We loaded and fired as we ran."

As the pursuing Union troops entered the wheat field, they encountered a Confederate line supported by three batteries. Captain W. Irving Hodgeson, commander of the Washington Artillery of New Orleans, held the center artillery position. He wrote, "we poured some 60 rounds into the enemy, who continued to advance upon us."

According to one of the gunners, Hodgeson had ordered the cannon to withdraw, but five minutes too late

Like the Washington Artillery, the Crescent Regiment was from New Orleans, Louisiana, the Crescent City. (cm)

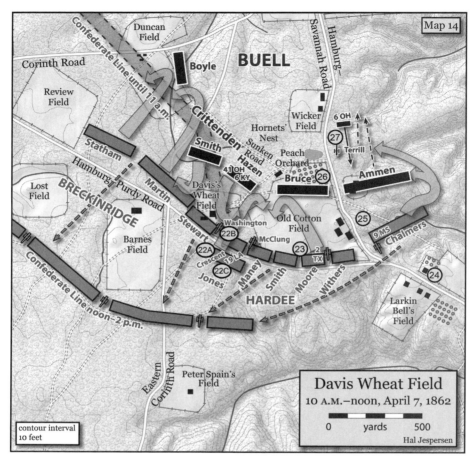

Davis Wheat Field

10 A.M.–noon, April 7, 1862

0   yards   500

contour interval
10 feet

Hal Jespersen

DAVIS WHEAT FIELD— Confederate troops under Gen. John C. Breckinridge hoped to continue with the success of the first day and complete the victory by initiating an offensive here, but instead ran into stiff resistance from fresh troops of Union Gen. Thomas L. Crittenden of Buell's army in the area of the Hornets' Nest and were eventually driven back and called upon to serve as the rearguard of the army.

for it to be carried out. "The balls were falling around us like hail," declared battery member John Pugh, "and before we could get ready [to withdraw] three horses at my piece and the same at two others were killed, our sergeant was killed and Lieut[.] Slocomb wounded, and we had to run leaving these three pieces on the field."

One of the artillery officers ran up to the nearby Crescent Regiment and the 19th Louisiana, which were both on the other side of the Hamburg-Purdy Road behind the cannon. "For God's sake, boys," pleaded the officer, "hurry up or our battery is gone!" The Union advance continued "until within some 20 yards of us," according to Hodgeson, and then the Confederate infantry support "gallantly came to our rescue, charging the enemy at the point of the bayonet."

The Union brigade of Col. William B. Hazen pursued Martin's Confederates across Davis's wheat field until it "found another line opposing"—the line including the Washington Artillery. "We pushed directly up to the mouths of the guns," Hazen recalled, "which were manned till the cannoneers were cut down by my men." Colonel Walter C. Whitaker, commanding the 6th Kentucky Union regiment of Hazen's brigade, reported that he "cut down one of the cannoneers with a bowie-knife," which had been "taken from a Texan who was captured by Private Brown, . . . a boy, who fought gallantly."

The Union troops continued on until "we were opened upon with grape from a battery on our left flank, creating considerable havoc," declared Hazen. A pair of cannon from McClung's Tennessee Battery to the east delivered that menacing fire. "The pursuit was here discontinued," Hazen lamented. The best the Union soldiers could do at this point was to temporarily disable the cannon by cramming mud into the vents at the rear of the gun—so it could not fire until cleaned out—and then retreat back across the field.

Richard L. Pugh of the Washington Artillery recalled, "The enemy came up to and even passed" three cannon that the gunners did not have time to withdraw before the Union attack reached them, "almost routing the Crescent regiment." (loc)

The Washington Artillery lost twenty horses in the melee. When the battery eventually retreated from this position, it made sure to withdraw the guns from the battlefield, though a lack of horses meant leaving three caissons, a wagon, and a forge.

After the Union attack was halted, the battery was saved, and the boys in blue forced to withdraw, the Crescent Regiment dashed after them. The regiment pursued the retreating Union troops into the brush on the far side of the field. Waiting Union reserves there stopped the gray soldiers cold, sending them reeling back across Davis's wheat field.

After the Washington Artillery finally withdrew from its position, fighting continued a bit longer before the Union army finally took the ground. Confederates in this sector withdrew down the Eastern Corinth Road to Prentiss's camps for one more stand on the battlefield before finally receiving the order to retreat to Corinth.

*   *   *

On the first day of the battle, General William J. Hardee had assumed command of all troops on the Confederate left, where many of his own troops were concentrated. But the exigencies of battle resulted in Hardee directing troops on the opposite end of the battlefield on the second day of fighting. Hardee found himself on a portion of the field with which he was unacquainted and leading troops with whom he was unfamiliar—troops equally unfamiliar with him.

When Col. John C. Moore, a West Point graduate

Though the 41-year-old John C. Breckinridge served as a major during the Mexican War, his unit saw no combat. His high military position was due to his political prominence. Breckinridge was the vice president in James Buchanan's administration, and he ran for the presidency on the Southern Democrat ticket when the party split in the contentious 1860 election won by Lincoln. (na)

At the age of 46, William Hardee was a West Point graduate with a 23-year career in the U.S. Army who had written the infantry tactics manual used widely by both sides during the Civil War. In the course of dealing with charges against Moore, it was reported that after being ridiculed, Moore's 2nd Texas had turned around and fired a volley over the heads of Hardee and his staff, and then went back to fighting. As it turned out, that incident occurred after Hardee had criticized some other regiment which—as with the 2nd Texas—was not accepting of their reprimand. (loc)

and leader of the 2nd Texas, received an order from an unknown general, he asked the identity of the stranger and learned that it was Hardee. Moore was to cooperate in Breckinridge's assault. "Before the advance was ordered," recalled Moore, "we were told that the brigade was to act as a support to General Breckinridge, who was engaging the enemy in front, and while advancing we were warned again and again by one or more staff officers not to fire on our friends in front."

Moore indicated that "after advancing some 200 yards a large force was seen in our front and to the right, but in a thick woods. This force was still believed to be our friends, and the caution again and again given not to fire, as they were Breckinridge's men."

The troops in front of Moore were not Breckinridge's Confederates, though, but Union forces in Nelson's division of Buell's army. "The greater part of the Second Texas passed over an open field," wrote Moore, noting that "the enemy, from the shelter in the woods, now poured into the whole line a most murderous fire." Sam Houston, Jr., the son of the former president of the Republic of Texas, recalled "The fence before us became transformed into a wall of flame." Houston was wounded near the groin on that day.

Being forbidden to return fire, the result was predictable. Moore lamented that his "whole line soon gave way from right to left in utter confusion."

Hardee sent staff officer Capt. William Clare, to rally Moore's men. When Clare returned, reported Hardee later, the Texans "swore they would not return to the field, and when told that [Hardee] would call them a 'pack of cowards,' said they did not care a damn what [Hardee] might call them." The men of the 2nd Texas understandably felt justified in refusing to obey orders from officers who not only had demonstrated a gross ignorance of troop positions but who were also unable to grasp that they had made a mistake.

At Davis's Wheat Field

Face the road and the direction that the cannon near the red tablet are pointing, looking north across the field. This is where Col. John D. Martin's men advanced—ahead of you—across Davis's wheat field.

Walk across the Hamburg-Purdy Road to the cannon and red oval tablet for the Washington Artillery position (stop 22B). Here the Washington Artillery held the center artillery position.

Turn around and walk back across the Hamburg-Purdy Road and to your left front to the monument for the Crescent Regiment (stop 22C).

With the monument to your back, look into the field. As the survivors of the Crescent Regiment regrouped after their counterattack, they noticed a wounded comrade who had collapsed before reaching the relative safety of the south side of the field. Lieutenant Seth Field and three others ran out with a blanket to retrieve the man. The soldier, "Sam," had been shot in the back, the bullet exiting just above his groin. The four rescuers took him to an ambulance, where the lieutenant expressed the hope that Sam would survive this seemingly mortal wound. But the wounded man replied, "Ah, Lieut., I believe they have got me this time." Sam died before he reached a field hospital and was buried.

Sam's brother David sought to learn the fate of his wounded sibling. David found the doctor who had recovered the effects from his brother's body and confirmed his worst fears. "It is my sad task to transmit the unwelcomed news that our poor brother Sam is no more," David wrote to some of his sisters. One of his sisters most likely learned of her brother's death from some other source, for the family was one of many torn apart by the Civil War. The dead Confederate soldier's full name was Samuel Todd. He was the oldest half-brother to the first lady of the United States, Mary Todd Lincoln.

Many families—even the family of the President of the United States—were torn apart by the Civil War. Mary Lincoln's half-brother Samuel was killed at the age of 32 near the Davis wheat field. Newspapers across the South used Todd's death as an opportunity to ridicule the first lady. The Macon Daily Telegraph wrote that Sam "died in defense of his country against the hireling invaders who the husband of his sister, Mrs. Abraham Lincoln, sent to desolate our country and dishonor our people." (uktc)

➤ **TO STOP 23**

Continue driving east on the Hamburg-Purdy Road. Go 0.4 mile to a gravel pull-off on the right of the road. On the left side of the road at this point are cannon astride a red rectangular tablet memorial to Statham's brigade. Beyond it is a field with a cabin on the far side.

At Sarah Bell's Old Cotton Field

Look ahead down the road. About 0.1 mile away on the left side of the road is the Texas monument—you will drive past it later. Walk across the road and look into the field toward the cabin. This is Sarah Bell's old cotton field.

Though Moore's men formed up near the Texas monument to your right, their course across Sarah Bell's field is uncertain. The "large force" to Moore's front and right might have been in the woods near the cabin.

➤ **TO STOP 24**

Continue driving down the Hamburg-Purdy Road for 0.5 mile, noting the Texas monument along the way. After passing a cannonball pyramid at the far side of a small field to your left, turn left on the next road. Drive back to the parking area by the cannonball pyramid.

The Texas monument is carved from red Texas granite. (gam)

CHAPTER THIRTEEN

April 6, 1862—late morning to mid-afternoon

*Note that this chapter is devoted to
the fighting on the first day of the battle.*

Probably no other brigade in the Union army has had its role in the battle of Shiloh interpreted to such extremes as the one commanded by Col. David Stuart. Some historians have declared that Stuart's brigade performed horribly and broke after a very short fight, while others have challenged that view and touted the merits of the brigade's prolonged stand.

Johnston's initial plan of battle called for sweeping around the Union left flank and driving the enemy northwest into the swamps of Owl Creek. When the Confederates drove Prentiss's division from its camps on April 6, Johnston may have thought that he had gained that Union left. But when Confederate engineer Capt. Samuel H. Lockett advised Johnston of yet another Union force beyond Prentiss's left—Stuart's brigade—the army commander altered his plans. Johnston refocused on the true Union flank.

Stuart was a lawyer and railroad solicitor with no military background. Positioned on the extreme Union left, he faced numerous disadvantages. Although part of Sherman's division, Stuart's brigade fought virtually on its own with no support and no practical advice from Sherman because the remainder of the division on the far Union right was fighting for its life between Shiloh Church and Jones Field two miles away. The battery originally attached to the brigade had been reassigned just the day before the battle, leaving Stuart without any artillery support of his own.

Stuart's brigade was assigned to defend the Hamburg Road and its crossing of Lick Creek. Even after Stuart realized that the sounds of combat on the morning of April 6 meant that heavy fighting had erupted to the west, he did not waiver from his original task of staying put to guard the Lick Creek Ford approach to the Union camps. Stuart set up

Sherman wisely posted his brigades to cover three of the four roads leading into the Union camps from the south and west, while Prentiss covered the fourth road. That arrangement, however, left David Stuart's brigade dangerously isolated from the remainder of the division. (gam)

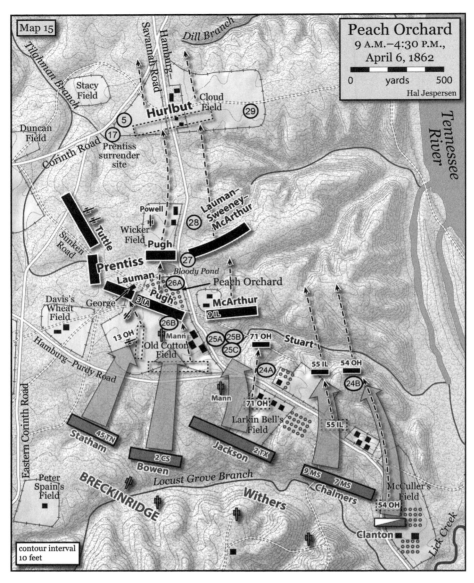

Peach Orchard
9 A.M.–4:30 P.M.,
April 6, 1862

0   yards   500

Hal Jespersen

Map 15

PEACH ORCHARD—Confederate Gen. A. S. Johnston's personal leadership was evident in this sector of the battlefield as he oversaw the critical aspect of his plan to turn the Union left flank. Johnston inspired and lead his troops in the assault that drove Union troops from the Peach Orchard, but he was mortally wounded in the attack.

a heavy picket line along Locust Grove Branch, a tributary of Lick Creek, and arrayed his main line overlooking the valley.

The main Union line in this phase of the battle was in the Sunken Road. The division of Stephen Hurlbut occupied the Sunken Road and part of the Hornets' Nest one-half mile to the right and rear of Stuart's position. One of W. H. L. Wallace's brigades, under Brig. Gen. John McArthur, sent to reinforce the Union left, had gone into a position about a quarter of a mile behind Stuart. It might have been more prudent for Stuart to fall back and form on either McArthur or Hurlbut, but Stuart resolved to carry out his orders and attempted to defend a position he could not possibly hold.

Johnston sent two brigades, numbering 4,500 men and supported by two batteries, against Stuart's 2,100 men unsupported by any artillery. About 11:00 a.m., the Confederates began driving in Stuart's pickets, and by 11:30 a.m., the gray soldiers switched targets from Stuart's picket line to his main line.

The 71st Ohio on Stuart's right in Larkin Bell's field broke under the artillery fire. Lieutenant Colonel Barton S. Kyle was mortally wounded while attempting to rally the men. "His fall had a most disheartening effect upon the entire regiment, by whom he was greatly esteemed," wrote Col. Rodney Mason, "the regiment having been recruited and organized by him." Some of the men in the 71st Ohio shifted to the left and linked up with the other two regiments of the brigade, while the bulk of the regiment headed toward the rear. Stuart reported, "I saw nothing more of the Seventy-first Regiment through the fight."

It was commonly believed that the regiment had shamefully run away. Though Stuart would not realize it, the majority of the 71st Ohio retired only about 200 yards, where they reformed and provided valuable service protecting the right flank of Stuart's other two regiments, which also fell back and took up a second position.

The 54th Ohio was first positioned behind a fence on the northern end of the McCuller Field, looking over an orchard, where it met the attack of James R. Chalmers's brigade.

"My line moved on across the orchard in most perfect order and splendid style," boasted Chalmers, "and to my great surprise not a shot was fired until we came within about 40 yards of the fence." The Confederates then overwhelmed the 54th Ohio. Benjamin F. Wilkinson, of Chalmers's 7th Mississippi recalled, "As they retreated I gave it to one old blue belly about where his suspenders crossed sending him to eternity."

Since this was the second engagement of the day for Chalmers's men, having earlier helped turn some of Prentiss's men out of Spain Field, the Confederates were low on ammunition and had to pause until ammunition wagons caught up with them. Some also looted Stuart's captured camps. That suspension of the fight gave the 54th Ohio an opportunity to retreat to a stronger second position. Together with the 55th Illinois to their right, these two regiments took superb advantage of the rugged terrain between Larkin Bell's field and the Tennessee River. Although all of Stuart's regiments had hastily fled from their first positions after a short fight, they would each put up a lengthy, desperate fight along the steep ravines at their second deployment.

A one-term congressman from Detroit, 46-year-old David Stuart was appointed a brigadier general in November, 1862, but resigned shortly after the U.S. Senate rejected his nomination in March 1863. Sherman hoped that Stuart might "return to the colors," but Stuart instead resumed the practice of law. (wc)

The landscape provided Union troops with excellent protection. "The men would drop down the hill to load, and crawl up to the top to fire," explained Lt. Elijah Lawrence, of the 55th Illinois, "in almost every case taking deliberate aim, with good effect." The Confederates also took advantage of the terrain. Wilkinson indicated that his 7th Mississippi "fought like Indians behind trees, logs, lying down behind the ridges, or hills."

Brigadier General John K. Jackson's 2nd Texas also fought on the steep slopes as well. J. H. Cravy noted that he had "seen the blood flowen down the sides of the hilles like water." Jackson's brigade had gained the ravine behind Stuart's right flank, while another problem also presented itself to the Union forces: "Our ammunition gave out," wrote S. B. Yeoman, an officer in the 54th Ohio, "and they were trying to flank us, which compelled us to leave the field." About 2:00 p.m., Stuart issued orders to withdraw.

One of the first tent hospitals of the war was established in this area, and Union Gen. Nelson cited "the admirable hospital arrangements adopted by Dr. [Bernard J. D.] Irwin. . . . They will be found as nearly perfect as the circumstances would allow." Wounded soldiers who could be transported were sent by boats to recovery hospitals in northern cities such as St. Louis, Missouri; Cincinnati, Ohio; and Cairo, Illinois. (bl)

Stuart's men suffered severely falling back across the ravine to where they planned to form their next position. "It was like shooting into a flock of sheep," Maj. F. Eugene Whitfield of the 9th Mississippi thought, also writing, "I never saw such cruel work in the war."

The remnants of Stuart's brigade reunited on a ridge to the north, where the now-wounded Stuart turned command over to Col. T. Kilby Smith of the 54th Ohio. Atop that northern ridge, a staff officer of Grant's arrived with orders for the brigade to withdraw, resupply ammunition, and take a new position supporting artillery along Grant's Last Line.

Admittedly, Stuart's men broke when first under fire, and one of the regiments was inaccurately believed to have fled from the battlefield. But the majority of the brigade reformed, and though outnumbered about two to one, was able to hold the Confederates off for more than two hours by making excellent use of the terrain, fighting until their ammunition was nearly exhausted. Most historians agree that Stuart's men performed admirably at the battle of Shiloh.

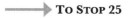

At Bell's Field

Walk to the orientation station (stop 24A) where markers face opposite directions—one facing north addressing a field hospital established here and one facing south describing the fighting at this location. Notice the 71st Ohio monument to the north, then turn to face south. The open ground across the Hamburg Road in front of you is Larkin Bell's field, where Col. David Stuart's men were posted on Prentiss's left.

The ground slopes down to Locust Grove Branch just beyond the field. The Hamburg Road crossed Lick Creek at a ford 1 mile to your left front.

The field hospital area sits just to the rear of Stuart's headquarters monument. (gam)

To appreciate the terrain utilized by the men on Stuart's left, take a 0.6 mile round trip walk. Walk back down the entrance road—to the east. Where the paved road makes a 90-degree bend to your right, continue walking straight down a gravel road. In about 50 yards, where a trail to the 55th Illinois monument forks to the left, keep going straight down the road. Continue walking another 115 yards to the 54th Ohio monument (stop 24B).

The initial position of the 54th Ohio was about one-quarter of a mile in advance of the monument, which is located at their second position. The 54th Ohio utilized the ridge for protection while their main line was, in fact, to the rear of this monument. After the battle, the survivors returned to bury their men where they fell, along the lip of the ravine. Notice the burial place marker and the ravine behind the monument.

➤ **TO STOP 25**

Return back down the gravel road and the paved entrance road to your vehicle. Exit the parking area and turn right onto the Hamburg Road. Almost immediately veer right again onto the Hamburg-Savannah Road. Drive 0.15 mile and turn right into the parking area for Johnston's death site.

The monument to the 54th Ohio shows the unusual Zouave uniform worn by the regiment. Modeled after the uniform worn by elite French troops during the recent Crimean War of 1853-56, several Civil War units selected the unique uniform, which traditionally included a fez as its headgear and red baggy pants. (gam)

C.S.

GENERAL ALBERT SIDNEY JOHNSTON

COMMANDING

THE
CONFEDERATE ARMY

WAS MORTALLY WOUNDED HERE
AT 2:30 P.M., APRIL 6, 1862,

DIED IN RAVINE, 50 YARDS
SOUTH-EAST, AT
2:45 P.M.

The Death of Albert Sidney Johnston

CHAPTER FOURTEEN

April 6, 1862—late morning to mid-afternoon

*Note that this chapter is devoted to
the fighting on the first day of the battle.*

Evidently to assure that his battle plan to turn the Union left flank was executed properly, Albert Sidney Johnston had stayed with the right of his army nearly from the start of the battle. About noon, Chalmers moved across the rough terrain beyond Stuart's camp, and Johnston realized that he had finally reached the Union left flank. "That check-mates them," the army commander declared. Major Edward Munford of Johnston's staff replied that the general "must excuse so poor a [chess] player for saying he could not see it." Even during the stress of battle, Johnston appreciated the humor and laughed. "Yes sir, that mates them," he reiterated.

While Chalmers had been struggling to pry Stuart out of his position, two brigades of Breckinridge's reserve corps, under Brig. Gen. John S. Bowen and Col. Winfield S. Statham, as well as the portion of Jackson's brigade not engaged with Stuart, had been under the very eye of Johnston (see Map 15 on page 128). Their opponent was the division of Brig. Gen. Stephen Hurlbut, posted in the north side of a cotton field belonging to Sarah Bell, and the brigade of Brig. Gen. John McArthur, east of the Hamburg-Savannah Road.

Breckinridge's men had attacked the Hurlbut-McArthur line several times, but the battle had settled into a static, stand-up fight in which both sides blazed at one another for nearly an hour. About 2:00 p.m., Johnston decided that the time had come to break the impasse. Johnston ordered a charge, but Breckinridge reported that he could not get his men to advance.

Johnston responded, "Then, I will help you. . . . We can get them to make the charge." Staffers were dispatched to different units. "Go to the extreme right," Johnston

The bullet that struck Johnston's right leg was fired from a .577 Enfield rifle. Although the Union army used this weapon at Shiloh, some 10,000 of these British-made rifles were imported and distributed to Confederate troops just prior to the battle. The shot that took Johnston's life was possibly fired by a Confederate soldier. (gam)

Wartime Tennessee Governor Isham G. Harris served as a volunteer aide to Johnston at Shiloh. Harris had been sent by Johnston to deliver a message to a Confederate unit to deal with a menacing Union artillery battery and had returned to report back to the general when he found Johnston at the site of the mortuary monument. (loc)

instructed Tennessee Governor Isham G. Harris, "and lead the Tennessee regiment stationed there"—meaning the 45th Tennessee of Statham's brigade.

Johnston then took the tin cup he had acquired from the 18th Wisconsin camp near Spain Field and rode along the battle line tapping the bayonets of his troops with the cup, and saying, "These men must do the work." Johnston also instructed Bowen's brigade: "Men of Missouri and Arkansas, the enemy is stubborn. I want you to show General Beauregard and General Bragg what you can do with your bayonets and tooth picks" ("Arkansas tooth picks" being a nickname for the Bowie knife).

Breckinridge's men, who moments earlier had rebuffed orders to attack, were now motivated by their army commander and ready to renew the fight. When Johnston yelled, "I will lead you!" the men let out a cheer "which rose high above the din of battle," and then vaulted ahead toward the Union line. The attack was a brilliant success. The Union line only "stood two fires when they took to their heels in real Bull Run style."

The army commander was in the thick of the fight. Johnston admitted to Harris, "Governor, they came very near putting me *hors de combat* in that charge," and showed him how a bullet ruined the sole on one of his boots. Soon Johnston sent Harris off again on yet another mission—delivering an order to Statham's brigade—after which the governor returned to report back to the army commander.

*   *   *

When Harris returned from Statham's brigade, he found Johnston, mounted on his horse, close to a large oak tree. Captain W. L. Wickham, an aide to Johnston, remembered that "Gov. Harris rode up, and said to Gen. Johnston that his order to silence or capture a battery had been executed." Harris recalled, "just at this moment the Genl sank down in his saddle leaning over to the left[.] I instantly put my left arm around him pulling him to me saying 'Genl are you wounded?' He said 'yes and I fear seriously.'"

While Harris supported the general's right side, Wickham did the same on his left. Wickham suggested taking the general to a ravine farther to the rear. "As we rode along Gen. Johnston fainted, and bridle-reins fell from his hands," witnessed Wickham.

Harris described the ride that the three horsemen made after leaving the oak tree: "We guided his horse from the crest of the hill to the ravine, where we lifted him from his horse [and] laid him upon the ground." Harris searched in vain on Johnston's torso for the fatal wound. Then they

Johnston's death at this site contributed to the criticism of his chosen place on the battlefield. Many have argued that when Johnston went to the battle front he not only abdicated army command to Beauregard, who was left to direct troops into action from the rear, but that his death substantiated the belief that an army commander needed to be in a place of safety in order to assure consistent army leadership. However, especially given the opposition to Johnston's plan by key subordinates on the eve of battle and again on the morning of the fight, his presence at the front was essential to assure that his plan to turn the Union left flank was properly executed. Furthermore, Johnston's ability to motivate green troops was demonstrated time and time again, when efforts by other major subordinates to do so had failed. (gam)

discovered a wound on the back of Johnston's right leg, just above his tall boot.

Colonel William Preston, brother of Johnston's first wife, was serving on Johnston's staff and discovered the small cluster of men gathering around the general in the ravine. Later, staff officer Lt. George W. Baylor found what he called "as sad a group as ever assembled on a battlefield." Baylor saw "Preston was kneeling and holding Gen. Johnston's head. . . ." And, "[b]ecoming cramped with the position, he [Preston] asked me to relieve him, which I did," wrote Baylor.

Baylor leaned over Johnston and sought to determine his degree of consciousness. "General, do you know me?" Baylor asked. "My tears were falling on his face, and his frame quivered for a moment," recollected Baylor, "then he opened his eyes, looked me full in the face, seeming to comprehend, and close them again." Johnston had died. It was then about 2:30 p.m.

Nine hours into his first day commanding an army in battle, Johnston was dead. Harris rode to Beauregard at Shiloh Church, informing him at about 3:00 p.m. that he was now in charge of the army.

At the Site of Johnston's Death

Walk out to the island of thin trees between the Johnston mortuary monument and the Hamburg-Savannah Road. Stand at a point nearly opposite a small black marker on the other side of the road—you may not be close enough to read it, but the marker denotes the "Sarah Bell Cotton Field"(stop 25A). In the ravine on the south side of the field, Johnston rallied his men, admonishing them to use their bayonets, before his men made their successful attack across

The tablet at the place where Johnston expired contains an account of Johnston's last moments by Gov. Isham G. Harris. (cm)

this field to drive the Union troop from its position near the north end of the field.

Walk over to the mortuary monument. After delivering an order for the general, Governor Harris returned to Johnston. Harris indicated that he found the general reeling in his saddle at this location (stop 25B).

Face the mortuary monument, then turn to your right and walk down the trail into the ravine for 50 yards to a large red tablet. Harris later identified this point as the location where they laid Johnston (stop 25C).

After first being interred in one of the St. Louis Cemeteries in New Orleans, Johnston was buried in the Texas State Cemetery in Austin beneath this solemn recumbent statue of him within a white, gothic, chapel-like structure. (gam)

Johnston himself may not have even been aware that he had been shot. He had been wounded in the right hip during a pistol duel, on February 5, 1837, with Felix Huston (Huston had felt his honor challenged when Johnston was named to replace him as the senior general in the Texan Army). The wound had damaged Johnston's sciatic nerve, and he had lost sensitivity to heat, cold, and pain

In 1896, then U.S. Senator Isham Harris went to the Shiloh Battlefield to help the historians at the new park mark the location where he had discovered the faint Gen. Johnston, slumping in his saddle. The park staff placed a wooden marker on a tree to identify the site. Even though the tree selected for the sign was likely just a sapling at the time of the battle, a legend grew that it was the tree that Johnston was under when Harris found the wounded general. Even after the tree died in the 1960s, the lore of the tree's significance was so strong that efforts were made to support and protect the stump of the tree. Its removal from the battlefield in 2001 was controversial to those who misunderstood the true saga of the tree. (nps)

in that leg. Johnston simply may not have felt any pain when he was shot and may not have known he was hurt until he grew faint. Treated immediately, it might have been possible to stop the bleeding, but Johnston had already lost too much blood by the time anyone became aware of the wound.

Johnston's death has generated much debate: about the proper place of an army commander in battle, about how he might have conducted the remainder of the battle of Shiloh, and about whether he would have fulfilled his early reputation as the top field commander in Confederate service. Students of the Civil War have long pondered these questions, and forever will.

------▶ TO STOP 26

Exit the parking area and turn right onto the Hamburg-Savannah Road. Drive 0.2 mile and turn left into the parking area for the Peach Orchard.

CHAPTER FIFTEEN

April 6, 1862—mid-morning to mid-afternoon

*Note that this chapter is devoted to
the fighting on the first day of the battle.*

The Union troops that the Confederates were assaulting at the time of Johnston's wounding had begun the first day of the battle near their camps closer to Pittsburg Landing when desperate pleas for help streamed in from the outlying Union divisions. Division commander Brig. Gen. Stephen Hurlbut sent one brigade to Sherman's assistance and then, with his other two brigades—some 4,400 men—moved south in line of battle down the Hamburg-Savannah Road to succor Prentiss.

By the time Hurlbut's men reached Sarah Bell's cotton field, they had already encountered many of Prentiss's panicked men heading for the rear. Hurlbut's troops could also see Confederate cannon in Prentiss's camp one-half mile to the south, and Confederate shells greeted the Union soldiers as they entered the field about 9:00 a.m. Too late to save Prentiss, Hurlbut aligned his men to await the inevitable Confederate advance (see Map 15 on page 128).

Hurlbut, then 46-years-old, was a lawyer and politician with an earned reputation for being unscrupulous. Though without military training, Hurlbut performed well as a soldier at Shiloh. He got off to a rocky start, however.

Hurlbut selected an awkward location for his initial position. Instead of utilizing as much of the open Sarah Bell Field as possible to provide his men with a good field of fire on approaching Confederates, he first posted his men on the far side of the field with virtually no space between the Union position and the woods in front of them.

Even as Hurlbut's men were forming into this position, complications developed. When Confederate artillery opened fire on Hurlbut's men, one of the first shells struck and killed the horse of Col. Nelson Williams, and the concussion from the explosion of the shell rendered him

With Bragg soon taking over this sector of the battlefield after the death of Johnston—his mortuary monument now stands in the distance—the Confederates did not pursue Federals after their Peach Orchard position fell and did not immediately try to wrestle Pittsburg Landing from the Union army. Instead, the Confederates directed their attention toward slicing in behind the Hornets' Nest and contributing to the capture of the 2,200 men of Prentiss and Wallace. (gam)

As a native of Charleston, South Carolina, serving in the Union army, and as a corrupt politician, the background of the 46-year-old Stephen Hurlbut marked him as a unique individual. His service as an officer in a South Carolina unit during one of the Seminole Wars, and his life as a lawyer and a politician in Illinois since the age of 30, help to explain how he came to command a division at Shiloh. (loc)

disabled for the remainder of the fight. Colonel Isaac C. Pugh succeeded Williams as the brigade went into position.

Another of those initial artillery rounds caused a different problem. The 13th Ohio Battery was posted in an exposed position near the apex of the angle in the line. One of the first shots fired at the battery struck a caisson with three full ammunition chests, causing a violent explosion, startling a team of horses that galloped wildly to the rear and frightening every one of the gunners as well. "All then left the battery without having fired a shot," observed a Union officer.

After staying in this unwieldy position for thirty minutes, Pugh saw Confederates moving toward his left—probably Jackson's brigade moving against Stuart—and withdrew his left unit to protect that flank. Hurlbut wisely withdrew both of his brigades further north at about 10:00 a.m.

After pulling his line back from his vulnerable initial position, Hurlbut formed an admirable battle line. His left formed on the south edge of a six-acre peach orchard—to become known as *the* Peach Orchard—then fully in bloom. Hurlbut's right angled back to the fence line along the Sunken Road and the cover of the woods. With much of his command aligned facing south across the large expanse of the Sarah Bell Field, Hurlbut offered his men an excellent field of fire with which to resist upcoming attacks.

The major drawback in Hurlbut's new line was that he had lost the tentative connection he had with Stuart's brigade, positioned to his left. That setback was substantively abated when the partial brigade of Brig. Gen. John McArthur arrived upon the field. McArthur commanded one of three brigades in W. H. L. Wallace's division. Like Hurlbut, Wallace had also received requests for support from both Sherman and Prentiss, and had also divided his command, sending troops to each. Wallace sent McArthur with his Scottish-clad brigade south where it slid into position east of the Hamburg-Savannah Road on Hurlbut's left about 10:30 a.m.

McArthur's brigade was the first unit along this line to be assaulted by the Confederates. When Chalmers and Jackson attacked Stuart, Jackson's line extended far enough to the west to bring his men in contact with McArthur as well. As tangible evidence of the intensity of the fighting on McArthur's front, his 9th Illinois suffered the highest numerical loss of any Union regiment on the battlefield of Shiloh: 366 from the regiment were killed, wounded, or missing. (John Cockerill, whose account is featured in the visitor center movie, participated in the 9th Illinois fight.)

Early in the afternoon, Confederates attacked the Peach Orchard and Sunken Road. Lieutenant Seymour

Thompson, in the 3rd Iowa of Williams's brigade, recalled one of the attacks:

A brigade leaped the fence, line after line, and formed on the opposite side of the field. It was a splendid sight, those men in the face of death closing and dressing their ranks, hedges of bayonets gleaming above them, and their proud banners waving in the breeze. Our guns, shotted with canister, made great gaps in their ranks, which rapidly closed, not a man faltering in his place. And now the field officers waved their hats. A shout arose, and that column, splendidly aligned, took the double quick and moved on magnificently.

Colonel John D. Martin, commanding Bowen's 2nd Confederate Infantry, reported, "We were led by General A. S. Johnston, who told us a few more charges and the day was ours." After entering into the Bell field, the regiment "crossed a deep ravine, driving their skirmishers before us. On reaching the top of a hill we were received with a destructive volley. . . . Simultaneously we returned their fire and charged ahead; they fled in confusion."

After Stuart's brigade had collapsed earlier in the day, the left flank of the Union army was in danger of being turned. Reinforcements from Wallace enabled Hurlbut to shift about half of his command east of the Hamburg-Purdy Road to augment McArthur's line, but even so, they still lacked the manpower to stop the Confederates. Hurlbut and McArthur both withdrew at about the same time, forming a new position to the rear. After making a brief stand north of the Peach Orchard, Hurlbut was able to form a more substantial position in Wicker Field, farther north along the Hamburg-Savannah Road.

Mann's Missouri Battery had originally been posted to the right of Stuart's brigade as his only artillery support, but after the 13th Ohio Battery abandoned their guns, Hurlbut decided he needed to replace them with Mann's Battery, withdrawing their cannon to this line of battle in front of the Peach Orchard. The cannon set up behind the ridge, using the crest as protection for both men and guns. During the time when Hurlbut's line successfully repulsed the initial attacks against it, the general wrote that "Mann's battery maintained its fire steadily, effectively, and with great rapidity. . . ." (gam)

The 9th Illinois was with the portion of MacArthur's brigade holding the isolated spot between Stuart's brigade to their left front, and Hurlbut's division to their right and rear. The regiment paid dearly, suffering more casualties than any other Union unit on the field. (gam)

One of the Confederates who fought on Sarah Bell's farm was A. H. Mecklin of the 15th Mississippi. After being engaged in a stand-up fight with the enemy in which he fired so much that his gun became too foul to load, his regiment was ordered to make a bayonet charge. "We ran forwards as rapidly as we could but being nearly exhausted we were unable to make but a little speed," Mecklin recalled. "The minie balls were falling thickly around us." (loc)

At the Peach Orchard

Go to the orientation station and look out into the Peach Orchard ahead of you (stop 26A).

A brigade under Col. Nelson G. Williams was originally posted on the far side of the field ahead, while Col. Jacob Lauman's first position was along the far side of the field to the right.

The 13th Ohio Battery was positioned on Lauman's left. From there, it broke and ran after the shell blew up its caissons. The battery was understandably disbanded after the battle for "disgraceful cowardice," contrasting sharply with so many other equally green units that somehow fought with courage and fearlessness during the horrific April 6 fight—a fight that would become the bloodiest day in American history at that time.

Walk to your right front through the Peach Orchard to the closest row of cannon for Mann's Missouri Battery (stop 26B). The monuments and cannon to your right and left mark Hurlbut's second position. This position fell during the Confederate attack launched just before Johnston was mortally wounded.

This cabin is the only surviving structure from the battlefield of Shiloh, though it is not in its original location. It stood in Perry Field, scene of fighting on the Union right predominantly on April 7. It was moved to the W. M. George farm shortly after the battle to replace one that had burned down at the same site during the battle. (gam)

➡ TO STOP 27

Exit the parking lot, turn left and drive just 0.1 mile to the pull-off on the right for the Bloody Pond.

The Bloody Pond

CHAPTER SIXTEEN

April 7, 1862—morning

Note that this chapter covers actions on the second day of the battle.

As the Union army stepped off on the morning of April 7 to retake the camps it had lost to the Confederates on the previous day, Brig. Gen. William Nelson's division on the left of Buell's army advanced on the Hamburg-Savannah Road. Nelson's men moved forward, coming under fire in Wicker Field about 8:00 a.m. Then Nelson waited for Crittenden's division, also of Buell's army, to catch up on his right.

Nelson came under artillery fire from several Confederate batteries, but he could not respond. When ordered to march from Savannah on the previous day, Nelson had felt that hauling cannon over muddy roads would significantly delay his arrival on the battlefield. Accordingly, he had purposely not brought his artillery along with him. Now, Nelson requested artillery support from other divisions of Buell's army.

One of the two batteries sent to Nelson was Capt. William R. Terrill's Battery H, 5th United States Artillery. Terrill, a 27-year-old West Point graduate from Virginia, decided to fight for the Union even though his state—and the rest of his family—supported the Confederacy. According to family tradition, William went to his father's home when the prospect of war loomed, and in the course of discussion concluded that he would stay in the United States army provided he would not be required to serve in his native Virginia.

Once Crittenden's men had advanced on line with Nelson's troops, the forward movement resumed. At about 10:00 a.m., Nelson's men reached the Peach Orchard and Sarah Bell's cotton field. Here the Union soldiers encountered some feeble Confederate attacks, including the advance of Colonel Moore with the 2nd Texas, carrying out its ill-advised orders from General Hardee (see Map 14 on page 122).

Water was a coveted commodity for the more than 100,000 soldiers who fought at Shiloh. While other bodies of water exist on the battlefield, none have become as famous as Bloody Pond. (cm)

Although some soldiers left accounts of other water sources on the battlefield being tainted with blood, no specific war-time accounts tell of the water being stained by blood at what would become known as the "Bloody Pond." The fame of the pond comes from a civilian account shared many years following the battle reporting its waters to be red from the blood of soldiers. (gam)

But when Nelson's men reached the woods on the far side of the field, they met stiffer Confederate infantry resistance—and a devastating flanking fire from a pair of batteries, including the Washington Artillery—in Davis's wheat field. In addition to the Confederate artillery pounding Nelson's right flank, Chalmers's infantry also struck his left. Soon the Union infantry fell back to Wicker Field, reforming in rear of its artillery, which had moved forward in conjunction with the infantry advance and went into battery near the area later known as "Bloody Pond."

The Confederates pursued, with Chalmers feeling that a critical moment in the battle had arrived: "Believing that one bold charge might change the fortunes of the day, I called upon my brigade to make one more effort, but they seemed too much exhausted to make the attempt, and no appeal seemed to arouse them. As a last resort I seized the battleflag from the color-bearer of the Ninth Mississippi Regiment, and called on them to follow. With a wild shout the whole brigade rallied to the charge, and we drove the enemy back."

As the Union infantry fled past Terrill's artillery—with Chalmers in hot pursuit—Nelson became concerned about the safety of the cannon. The division commander approached Lt. Col. Nicholas Anderson of the 6th Ohio to deliver special orders. "I have conferred upon your regiment the honor of defending this battery, the best in the service,"

Nelson shouted. "*It must not be taken!*" The 6th Ohio "came forward with alacrity," wrote Terrill. "They stood by me to the last."

Colonel Jacob Ammen led the brigade fighting on the east side of the Hamburg-Savannah Road. Probably recalling this phase of the battle, Ammen wrote, "On the rebels come with loud shouts, and when they are at the proper place the men of the [brigade] rise, the front rank fires, loads; the rear rank fires, &c. The rebels find the aim too accurate and the balls too numerous to continue the advance; they fall back, renew the attack repeatedly, but are each time repulsed by the brave men and officers under my command."

Grant had intended that portions of his battered army should serve as the reserve on April 7 and, at about noon, some of the troops that had fought so hard the previous day reinforced Nelson. The Union left advanced one more time, taking the Hamburg-Purdy Road beyond the Bell field about 2:00 p.m. as the Confederates retreated first to Prentiss's camps—and then to Corinth.

At Bloody Pond

Stand behind the cannon marking the position of Terrill's Battery. Looking in the same direction as the cannon are pointing, the Bloody Pond is visible across the Hamburg-Savannah Road to your right front. Wicker Field is 0.1 mile behind you.

Captain William R. Terrill was promoted to brigadier general; later, while rallying his brigade in the battle of Perryville, Kentucky, on October 8, 1862, he was mortally wounded by a shell fragment that tore his side. His brother, James B. Terrill, also would become a brigadier general and would be killed in action, except that his brother served in the Confederate army. James fell on May 30, 1864, during the battle of Bethesda Church, Virginia. Supposedly a monument was created containing the inscription: "This monument erected by their father. God only knows which was right."

➤ TO STOP 28

Drive 0.2 mile further, parking on the right at the pull-off on the far side of the next field at the Missouri monument.

Grant's Left Flank

CHAPTER SEVENTEEN

April 6, 1862, late afternoon—April 7, 1862, dawn

Note that this chapter covers actions on the first day of the battle and is a continuation of where we left off at the Peach Orchard (Chapter 15), with Hurlbut's withdrawal during the afternoon.

Just before Johnston's death, when his Confederates drove Hurlbut from the Peach Orchard, the Union men made a brief stand in the woods near Bloody Pond. The final attempt to maintain some semblance of a Union defense near the Hornets' Nest took place on the south side of Wicker Field. The main battle line extended into the woods on either side of the field (see Map 15 on page 128).

One of the four Union batteries supporting Hurlbut's position on Wicker Field was Battery F, 2nd Illinois Artillery, under the command of Capt. John Wesley Powell. This particular battery was aligned in the northwest corner of the field. Because the noise of battle often hampered the ability of men to hear verbal orders, artillerymen also relied upon visual signals. Powell indicated that he was in the act of raising his hands to communicate to his men that a gun was about to fire when "a musket ball struck my arm above the wrist which I scarcely noticed until I attempted to mount my horse." Powell's arm later was amputated.

The Union artillery and infantry units that fought there fell back about 4:00 p.m. They made another brief stand in Cloud Field—the next opening to the north, astride the Hamburg-Savannah Road—but Hurlbut could hold on no longer, and retreated to join other forces forming Grant's Last Line near the landing.

Confederate troops that all day had been trying to turn the Union left flank finally succeeded. They chose not to pursue Hurlbut further and did not immediately try to wrestle Pittsburg Landing from the Union army. Instead, the Confederates turned their attention to the capture of the Hornets' Nest (see Map 11 on page 84). The Confederates in this sector cut in behind the troops of Prentiss and W. H. L. Wallace, contributing to the capture of 2,200 men.

The loop trail to the Indian Mounds also leads to an overlook of the Tennessee River. (gam)

Shortly after the Confederates had secured the Hornets' Nest prisoners, some 8,000 Southern infantrymen lined up on south side of Dill Branch. They would test Grant's Last Line.

*   *   *

Just as Union forces earlier had effectively used streams as barriers to the Confederates in the defense of Union camps, so Grant also made skillful use of the terrain for his last line. The left end of Grant's Last Line was anchored on the Tennessee River and was posted behind Dill Branch (see Map 4 on page 16). Union artillery lining the ridge north of Dill Branch had an effective field of fire across the rain-filled ravine with its steep banks.

The loss of Powell's arm at Shiloh did not prevent the resilient officer from embarking upon one of the most physically demanding post-war careers. Powell became a prominent explorer and scientist and, in 1869, gained the distinction of being the first person to successfully navigate the treacherous Colorado River through the Grand Canyon. (loc)

Adding to the strength of the Union position, two advantageously positioned wooden gunboats of the Union navy—the Tyler and the Lexington—anchored at the mouth of Dill Branch. Throughout both days of the battle, the gunboats steamed up and down the edge of the battlefield seeking opportunities to help. About the time that Prentiss surrendered, the gunboats had shifted to the point where Dill Branch emptied into the Tennessee River, and it soon became apparent that the naval vessels were in a perfect position. The gunboats, together with the field and siege artillery making up Grant's Last Line, placed any Confederates who dared to enter the Dill Branch ravine in a deadly crossfire.

The extreme left flank of Grant's Last Line was positioned on a small knoll just north of where Dill Branch emptied into the Tennessee River.

Two batteries occupied the hill, situated to augment the Union gunboats in firing into the flank of attacking Confederates. Of the two batteries, the 8th Ohio Battery was a fresh unit, but the 1st Minnesota Battery of Prentiss's division had already been heavily engaged: first, in the struggle to hold the Union camps, and second, in the heart of the Hornets' Nest.

Minnesota artilleryman Henry S. Hurter indicated that on the evening of April 6 "we took our position on the hill overlooking the slough

Many of the ironclad gunboats of the Western Flotilla were undergoing repairs at the time of the battle of Shiloh. The most formidable boats in the flotilla had suffered damage during the battle of Fort Donelson, and deficiencies in the vessels that became evident in their maiden battles were also being corrected. But the heavy-duty gunboats were not needed at Shiloh as the timberclads Tyler and Lexington easily accomplished their missions. (loc)

through which the enemy was expected to make his last charge. We had five guns in position a short distance to the left of where Col. Webster had formed an immense battery."

Command of the 1st Minnesota had devolved upon Lt. William Pfaender, who reported, "The rebels knew that this last attack would decide the day, and at about six o'clock in the evening opened on us again . . . a few moments afterwards the pieces of the First Minnesota Battery joined in such a cannonade as has never before witnessed on the continent. It was really majestic and no army would have been able to take that position." Yet some of the Confederates did try to take the stronghold, and Hurter recalled, "when the enemy made the attempt he found the reception too hot and gave it up."

William Gwin, commanding the timberclad Tyler at Shiloh, later became a lieutenant commander in charge of the formidable ironclad Benton during the Chickasaw Bayou Campaign near Vicksburg, Mississippi. On December 27, 1862, just as Gwin stepped out of his iron-plated pilothouse, proclaiming "a captain's place was on his quarterdeck," a rifled projectile hit the right side of his chest, mortally wounding him. (loc)

Gen. James Chalmers explained what the Confederates faced as they tested the strength of Grant's ridge: "in attempting to mount the last ridge we were met by a fire from a whole line of batteries protected by infantry and assisted by shells from the gunboats. Our men struggled vainly to ascend the hill, which was very steep, making charge after charge without success, but continued to fight until night closed hostilities on both sides."

One of the Confederate brigades that moved against Grant's Last Line noticed the position held by the 1st Minnesota and 8th Ohio. Confederate Colonel John D. Martin wrote, "When within 300 or 400 yards of the river the enemy opened on us with their gunboats and two batteries in position near the river bank, which sounded terribly and looked ugly and hurt but few. Our men began to discover this fact. Being now nearly night, I fell back, by an order from General Bragg."

*   *   *

The order to withdraw had been passed down from General Beauregard, who decided to call off the attack. He believed that if the Union forces did not retreat during the night, the Confederates could complete the victory on the following morning. Beauregard then pulled his army back to the outlying Union camps in an attempt to escape the fire of the Union gunboats.

While darkness brought an end to traditional operations, the gunboats were called upon to carry out a primarily psychological mission. Grant understood that shelling the Confederate lines all night would cause the enemy to be uneasy, not knowing just if or when an artillery projectile might come crashing down upon their bivouac. It also sent positive notice to the Union troops: although they had been driven back all day, the shelling demonstrated that Union forces still possessed some powerful might and

James Chalmers, a 31-year-old lawyer who would have substantial Civil War service in Nathan Bedford Forrest's cavalry, had fought in Spain Field, and from Stuart's Camps to Wicker Field before reaching Dill Branch. Chalmers wrote of his attack on Grant's Last Line: "This was the sixth fight in which we had been engaged during the day, and my men were too much exhausted to storm the batteries on the hill, but they were brought off in good order...." (loc)

fighting spirit. From 9:00 p.m. to 1:00 a.m., the Tyler fired a round every ten minutes, then after 1:00 a.m., the crew of the Lexington took over the task.

Beauregard placed great emphasis on the importance of the Union navy support. Mistakenly thinking that the wooden Union vessels were actually protected with iron armor plating, Beauregard told his men following the battle: "You drove him from his camps to the shelter of his iron-clad gunboats, which alone saved him from complete disaster."

At the end of the first day of battle, Beauregard was still confident and sent a premature telegraph to President Jefferson Davis: "We this morning attacked the enemy in strong position in front of Pittsburg, and after a severe battle of ten hours, thanks be to the Almighty, gained a complete victory, driving the enemy from every position. Loss on both sides heavy, including our commander-in-chief, General A. S. Johnston, who fell gallantly leading his troops into the thickest of the fight."

On the morning of April 7, yet another consequence of Beauregard's decision to withdraw his troop the previous evening became apparent to those who understood the terrain at Shiloh. By pulling all the way back to the Union camps and by waiting until the sound of Union gunfire on the morning of April 7 before forming up their men, the Confederates were not able to establish their initial defensive line behind the considerable terrain features, such as Dill Branch. Though the Confederate army may well have been driven from the Shiloh battlefield on April 7 anyway, Confederates could likely have made the task even more costly to the Union forces if they had held or reestablished their advanced positions of the evening of April 6.

At Wicker Field

Confederate Gen. John S. Bowen, a Missouri resident at the outbreak of the war, was wounded in the neck early in the fight for Wicker Field on April 6. (gam)

The Missouri monument, near the pull-off, honors troops from the divided border state, listing units that served on both sides at Shiloh.

Walk back in the direction of Bloody Pond into Wicker Field. Walk until you can see an Illinois monument and two cannon across the field to your right. They represent Powell's Battery F, 2nd Illinois Artillery. Your location is in the northeast corner of the field; Powell's Battery was posted in the northwest corner.

The Native American farming community that built these mounds also traded with other distant communities. One of the most prominent artifacts recovered at the site was an effigy pipe, believed to come from the Cahokia Mounds in Illinois, near present day St. Louis. This artifact is currently on display at the Tennessee River Museum in Savannah, Tennessee. (gam)

⟶ TO STOP 29

Continue driving for 0.3 mile. In Cloud Field, turn right on Brown's Landing Road. Drive 0.2 mile and turn left into the parking area for the Indian Mounds pavilion and trailhead.

At the Indian Mounds

A part of what became the Shiloh battlefield was historically significant long before the Civil War. A forty-six-acre site high on a bluff overlooking the Tennessee River was an important political center for Native Americans living there about the year 1200.

The site contains seven large mounds of earth. On top of six rectangular mounds were governmental structures or temples or the homes of prominent residents. The one oval mound contained the burials of prominent inhabitants. Many smaller and much lower mounds indicate the locations of houses.

An exhibit shelter by the parking lot is also the trailhead of a 1.1-mile loop trail through the mounds with interpretive panels located along the footpath.

⟶ TO STOP 30

Exit back onto Brown's Landing Road and turn left. Drive 0.6 mile to Dill Branch.

At the Dill Branch Ravine

Each of the two Union timberclad gunboats were armed with two 32-pounder cannon, like the reproduction guns currently on display at the Dill Branch Ravine tour stop, as well as four 8-inch smoothbores. During the Confederate attack across Dill Branch against Grant's Last Line, Lt. Gwin reported, "Both vessels opened a heavy and well-directed fire on them, and in a short time, in conjunction with our artillery on shore, succeeded in silencing their artillery, driving them back in confusion." (gam)

The causeway constructed across Dill Branch Ravine was not here at the time of the battle. Unlike virtually all of the other cannon on the Shiloh battlefield, the cannon displayed at this tour stop are reproductions of naval guns similar to those that would have been used on the two wooden gunboats cruising the river. Today, the Tennessee River has been dammed at several places, and the river is about one-third wider than it would have been at the time of the battle. The Tennessee River flows north, the direction you have been traveling. With your back to the river, Grant's Last Line would be to your right, lining the north edge of Dill Branch.

Some 150 yards wide and up to 90 feet deep, the Dill Branch Ravine was predominantly clear of vegetation as local residents had cut down trees near the river, selling the wood as fuel for steamboats stopping at Pittsburg Landing, just one-quarter mile downriver.

→ **To Stop 31**

Continue driving 0.2 mile to Grant's Left Flank.

At Grant's Left Flank

One of the most controversial aspects of the battle of Shiloh surrounds Beauregard's order for the Confederate forces to fall back at the moment they tested Grant's Last Line. Many felt that the death of Johnston, just three hours earlier, deprived the Confederates of the leadership that would have continued to press the Confederate attack that had driven the Union forces from their every position that day. Advocates of this viewpoint feel that Johnston's ability to motivate troops would have been a decisive factor or that he would have been able better to consolidate the Confederate forces to launch a more massive attack than what did occur. They not only argue that Johnston would have attacked Grant's Last Line, but that he would have been successful in doing so, and that Grant would have been defeated before any of the Union reinforcements had arrived. This assessment contends that Confederate victory was nearly within the grasp of Johnston's army. The Confederate monument at Shiloh advocates this version of the battle of Shiloh.

But many hold another view of the situation. Taking into consideration the many hours that the Confederate army had been fighting that day, with all of its reserves already committed to the battle long before the attempt to take Grant's Last Line, some argue that the Confederates had assembled all of the troops they might reasonably expect to mass for a final attack. This faction concludes that it would have been too difficult for an organized body of troops to maintain enough cohesion to cross Dill Branch and still launch a substantive attack. Then, even if a massive number of troops could have made it across the ravine in a significant assault, the Confederates could not have overwhelmed the firepower of the fifty cannon, supported by infantry and two gunboats.

Though many feel that Beauregard made the proper decision in ending the fighting when he did, it also has been argued that he did so for the wrong reasons.

The monument and first pair of cannon encountered at this stop mark the position of the 8th Ohio Battery. The blue tablet and cannon beyond mark where the 1st Minnesota, Munch's Battery went into action.

Civil War artillery was most effective when used as a defensive weapon, and the Union cannon here and on Grant's Last Line, in conjunction with the terrain, created a nearly impregnable defensive position. (cm)

➤ TO STOP 32

Continue driving 0.1 mile to the pull-off for the Pittsburg Landing overlook.

Following Stop 32, the last tour stop, continue driving 0.1 mile to return to the visitor center to conclude the tour.

Pittsburg Landing
CHAPTER EIGHTEEN
April 8-11, 1862

The key to victory at Shiloh was possession of Pittsburg Landing. The Confederate objective was to cut off the Union army from its line of supplies passing through the landing and then trap the Federals against the swamps to the north. The Union army realized that, to have a chance at extending the battle into a second day, it needed to maintain a hold on the landing by the end of the first day's fighting. The failure of the Confederates to wrestle the landing away from their opponent deprived them of the opportunity of a complete victory at Shiloh, and it gave the Union army the chance to seize the initiative and ultimately turn a disastrous first day of the battle into a Union triumph.

In the aftermath of the battle, Pittsburg Landing was the scene of activity different from the hustle and bustle prior to the fight. Instead of virtually all of the river traffic bringing in troops and supplies, a substantial part of the commotion came from evacuating wounded for hospitals established at major river port cities to the north.

The Confederate equivalent to Pittsburg Landing was the supply base at Corinth. Unlike the Union's easy access to Pittsburg Landing, the defeated Confederates suffered a tedious trek of about twenty miles to transport their wounded to Corinth before they could be dispersed by train to other Southern cities.

On April 8, the day following the battle, Union troops pursued the Confederates to assure that they were indeed heading back to Corinth—not still in the vicinity of Shiloh poised for battle. Sharp skirmishing five miles southwest of Pittsburg Landing at a place known as Fallen Timbers convinced Union authorities that they had encountered only a rearguard, that the Confederate army had evacuated the battlefield, and that the battle of Shiloh was over.

The outcome of the engagement on Grant's Last Line was the key to determining the overall outcome of the battle. When the Union army held Pittsburg Landing, it nearly assured Union victory. (gam)

The losses on both sides were staggering. Officially the Confederates suffered 1,728 killed, 8,012 wounded, and 959 missing for a total loss of 10,699. Union losses, in both Grant's and Buell's armies, were reported as 1,754 killed, 8,408 wounded, and 2,885 missing, for a total of 13,047 casualties.

Some of the men in Nathan Bedford Forrest's small cavalry force got close enough to Pittsburg Landing on the evening of April 6 to observe the arrival of Buell's reinforcements. Forrest tried in vain that night to locate army headquarters to report his findings, or to convince any high-ranking general he could find, including Hardee, that Confederates needed to react to what he had discovered. Forrest was wounded in the final action of the battle at the engagement at Fallen Timbers. This picture is of the equestrian statue of Forrest that once stood over his grave in Memphis. (gam)

Along with the after-battle supplies coming into Pittsburg Landing were several governors of Northern states to visit the troops. One official visit ended in tragedy when Wisconsin Governor Louis P. Harvey fell into the river while stepping from one boat onto another; Harvey drowned there.

On April 11, Gen. Henry Halleck arrived at the landing to take command of the combined Union armies for the long-planned advance on Corinth. Additional Union forces converged on Pittsburg Landing, too, so Halleck led a force of some 125,000 soldiers to Corinth. By the end of April, a month-long siege began. The siege ended with Beauregard giving up the railroad crossing, barely offering a fight for what was largely an indefensible position. When Beauregard went on sick leave in June, President Davis replaced him with Braxton Bragg, who also proved deficient as an army commander. After Shiloh, the Confederacy searched in vain for a suitable commander of its western army. "When Sidney Johnston fell, it was the turning point of our fate," wrote Davis, "for we had no other to take up his work in the West."

Johnston contributed to the army the resolve to fight the battle of Shiloh when on the very eve of battle many of his subordinates wanted to return to Corinth. In an atmosphere where his corps commanders questioned the wisdom of the fight, Johnston placed himself on the critical right flank of the Confederate army to execute the turning of the Union left flank. When troops faltered in front of the Peach Orchard, he personally motived his men at the cost of his life. Though Johnston had made mistakes prior to Shiloh and did not execute a perfect battle at Shiloh, he had shown indisputable leadership, and considering his army was so inexperienced, he was able to gain some remarkable achievements at Shiloh.

It has often been said that when Johnston went to the front, he abdicated army command to Beauregard, and that Beauregard had a better grasp of the conduct of the battle than the army commander. Yet when Beauregard inherited the army, he saw fit to take his place at the front on the second day of the battle, often inspiring the men and overall playing a very similar role to the one Johnston filled on the first day at Shiloh.

For Grant, the memory of him as "Unconditional Surrender" Grant and the victor of Fort Donelson was short-lived. The public, politicians, and press in the North demanded to know whether Grant was surprised at Shiloh, and they were angered and shocked at the high casualty figures. Though the Union performance at the battle of Shiloh was hardly a model of precision, Grant displayed a perseverance to continue fighting while things were going terribly wrong and an aggressive disposition to turn the tide with a counterattack. This determination not to accept defeat would serve Grant and the Union cause well on multiple battlefields throughout the Civil War.

It was after Shiloh that Grant realized the type of war that would be required to bring the conflict to an end. Grant wrote in his memoirs, completed in 1885, "Up to the battle of Shiloh I, as well as thousands of other citizens, believed that the rebellion against the Government would collapse suddenly and soon, if a decisive victory could be gained over any of its armies." But after Shiloh, Grant conceded, "I gave up all idea of saving the Union except by complete conquest."

Between the gunboats of the U.S. Navy and the transports and supply ships of the U. S. Army Quartermaster Corps, an estimated 174 vessels were utilized in the Shiloh operations. At times boats were stacked up three deep at Pittsburg Landing as they waited to unload supplies or discharge troops. (gam)

By the time of the battle of Shiloh, the idea of a negotiated peace and a bloodless war had long been abandoned. The idea of a one-battle war had also been shattered. But the realization that the Civil War could produce a level of combat in which each side would sustain in excess of 10,000 casualties was realized for the first time at Shiloh. And, Grant's assessment after Shiloh that war would only come to an end via the "complete conquest" of the Confederacy was indeed true.

The legacy of Shiloh was that the war would cost more than anyone envisioned and that because the sides would fight with such intense commitment, the war could not end until one side or the other was completely and soundly defeated.

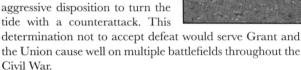

Lew Wallace's division initiated the fighting of April 7, 1862 by driving off a Confederate brigade and then setting up an artillery line here in north Jones Field. (gam)

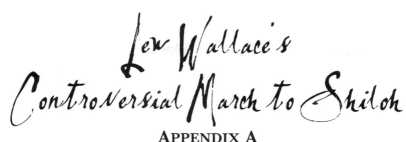

Lew Wallace's Controversial March to Shiloh

APPENDIX A

by Ryan T. Quint

Shortly after 7:00 p.m. on April 6, 1862, as dusk ended Shiloh's bloody first day of combat, Maj. Gen. Lew Wallace's three brigades of the Federal army's 3rd Division arrived near Pittsburg Landing. Ever since that day, Wallace's route to the battlefield has been plagued with controversy in the historiography of the war. What exactly happened to Wallace's roughly 7,500 men? How is it that a march of, theoretically, just under six miles that should have taken only a couple of hours instead turned into an all-day adventure?

Even during the battle, Maj. Gen. Ulysses S. Grant's staff members began to point fingers and accuse Wallace of being lost. This charge stuck to the Indiana-born commander, and he spent the rest of his life fighting the accusation, not succeeding entirely in his efforts. Historians latched onto the lost narrative, with James McPherson writing in the Pulitzer Prize winning *Battle Cry of Freedom* that "Wallace took the wrong road" and labeling his command a "lost division." Another writer hit harder, accusing Wallace of "an amazing display of incompetence" and of having "marched away from the battlefield." But there is a major problem with this kind of narrative: Lew Wallace was not, for a single moment, lost on April 6, 1862.

Explaining Wallace's decisions on April 6 starts just shy of a month earlier—on March 13, when his command arrived at Crump's Landing, five miles north of Pittsburg Landing. While Grant's other divisions encamped around Pittsburg Landing and the Shiloh Church, Wallace protected the Federal army's northern flank. In a move that would prove essential on April 6, Wallace set out to determine different approaches he could take to get from Crump's Landing to the right flank of the rest of the army near the church.

One of those approaches that Wallace focused his attention upon was the Shunpike. Under the heavy spring rains, the Shunpike had become a muddy bog, and Wallace ordered Maj. Charles Hayes to set about fixing the road and corduroying it—laying logs down to make an improved road surface. As Wallace wrote in his autobiography, "Somewhere in the last week of March, Major Hayes reported the work done; and to be certain of it, I rode with him and one [of] his companies . . . to Pittsburg Landing, and back again." Not only did Wallace know what road to take to get to the army, he had even been the one who ordered it prepared.

On the morning of April 6, Wallace awoke to a sentinel reporting sounds of a battle. Acting quickly, Wallace sent out orders for his three brigades to concentrate at Stony Lonesome, a point not far from the Shunpike. From Stony Lonesome, Wallace also had the choice of marching onto the Savannah-Hamburg Road (also known as the River Road), which would have carried his division directly to Pittsburg Landing. Before moving his

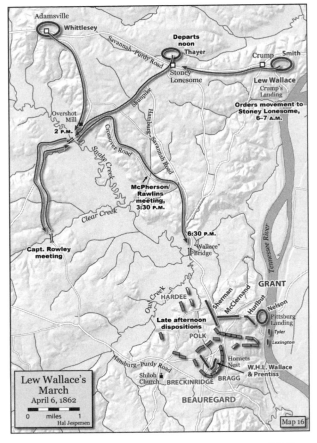

LEW WALLACE'S MARCH— Though Lew Wallace has been unfairly criticized as getting "lost" as he marched from his camp near Crumps Landing to the Shiloh battlefield, he was actually quite familiar with the road network and knew just where he was heading. Through the miscommunication from a written message that has been lost to history, Wallace was marching to assist Sherman on a portion of the battlefield that had fallen to the Confederates about two hours into the fight.

division toward the sound of the guns, however, Wallace needed to wait for word from Grant.

Grant was not with the army when the battle started but had instead spent his nights at Savannah, located upriver from Pittsburg Landing. Also waking up to reports of gunfire, Grant boarded a ship and began steaming his way south on the Tennessee River. He stopped at Crump's Landing between 8:00-8:30 a.m. and ordered Wallace to keep his division ready to move—an objective Wallace had already accomplished when he ordered his brigades to consolidate at Stony Lonesome. Grant told Wallace to wait for specific orders, while Grant moved ahead to Pittsburg Landing to get a feel for the battle. The man who would carry the orders to march, Capt. A. S. Baxter, delivered them to Wallace sometime between 11:00 and 11:30 a.m.

The crux of the controversial march to Shiloh and the charges of taking the "wrong" road stem from the exact wording of Grant's orders. Having been given verbal orders, John Rawlins, one of Grant's staffers, turned to Baxter and ordered the captain to deliver the order to Wallace.

At some point, Baxter wrote the order down on a scrap of paper. Captain Frederick Knefler, serving on Wallace's staff, subsequently lost the paper and later bemoaned that fact, writing to Wallace, "I feel confident that its production now, would conclusively demonstrate that you obeyed the command contained in it."

Two opposing views arose from the order. Grant and his staffers swore that Wallace was ordered to march to Pittsburg Landing via the Savannah-Hamburg Road. Wallace and his staff officers, however, pled that the paper contained different orders. For the remainder of his life, Wallace adamantly insisted that the order read, in part, "march and form [a] junction with the right of the army."

Even Baxter, writing in 1886 that Wallace was point-blank ordered to use the Savannah-Hamburg Road, may have been misremembering, because he wrote that Wallace replied that he "knew the road and had put it in good order." But as Wallace biographer Gail Stephens points out, "Wallace would never have said that if he had been ordered to take the River Road for he had made no repairs to it."

Because the paper was lost, the exact wording will forever be a controversy. Wallace's decision to use the Shunpike was not the result of being lost, or picking the wrong road, but because it made the most sense in following Grant's order. He spent almost the next forty-three years defending that choice.

This is not to say that Wallace made no mistakes on April 6. His first mistake came shortly after getting Grant's order: he paused for lunch. After waiting some three hours for orders and being visibly impatient, Wallace's decision to then allow his men half an hour to eat their rations is baffling.

By noontime, Wallace's three brigades swung onto the Shunpike and began to march toward the battlefield. As Wallace's men began their march, it was Grant's turn to get progressively more impatient, and he began to send a litany of staff officers to find the division. Captain William Rowley found Wallace's command, between 2:00 and 2:30 p.m., about five miles from its starting point at Stony Lonesome. Wallace explained to Rowley that he planned on bringing his division onto Sherman's right flank, to which Rowley responded, according to Wallace, "Great God! Don't you know Sherman has been driven back? Why, the whole army is within half a mile of the river and it's a question if we are not all going to be driven into it."

Wallace made the decision to turn his division around and find a new path to get to the army via Pittsburg Landing, and here he made his second mistake. Wallace had arranged his three brigades in the order that he had wanted them to deploy onto the battlefield, and instead of just having the rearguard become the vanguard of his column by about-facing, Wallace ordered his first brigade to counter-march along the entire length of the division. This caused a massive traffic jam as the soldiers tried to squeeze past each other on the Shunpike.

The terrible conditions of the paths that crossed overland and connected with the Savannah-Hamburg Road bogged the division in thick mud, delaying Wallace further. His men finally broke through the quagmire and marched onto the battlefield around 7:00 p.m., seven hours after they had left Stony Lonesome.

Wallace's isolated position here at Crump's Landing and points further west, while the remainder of the army was further upstream at Pittsburg Landing, was so his division could make excursions to the west, threatening or damaging the Mobile and Ohio Railroad. (bl)

But then Wallace fell victim to a scapegoating campaign launched in the wake of the battle of Shiloh. Facing the worst casualties ever seen by an American army up to that point, people began asking whether Grant were perhaps the wrong man for the job. Lew Wallace became the easy target of a false narrative about being lost, taking the wrong road. Grant's staff officers closed ranks to protect their commander. Trying to defend his name, Wallace eventually asked for a court of inquiry, but by that time Grant was a national hero; Wallace meekly withdrew the request and continued to serve the Union war effort. He commanded a patched-together force defending Washington, D.C., in the summer of 1864, along the banks of the Monocacy River, an action that became known as "The Battle that Saved Washington."

Wallace continued to defend his actions at Shiloh until his death on February 15, 1905. Historians have ever since continued to debate what exactly happened on the Shunpike on April 6, 1862.

RYAN QUINT *is a former park ranger at the Fredericksburg and Spotsylvania National Military Park and the author of* Determined to Stand and Fight: The Battle of Monocacy, *part of the Emerging Civil War Series.*

THE BATTLE OF SHILOH

ARMY OF THE TENNESSEE
Maj. Gen. Ulysses S. Grant

FIRST DIVISION: Maj. Gen. John A. McClernand
First Brigade: Col. Abraham M. Hare (w); Col. Marcellus M. Crocker
8th Illinois • 18th Illinois · 11th Iowa • 13th Iowa

Second Brigade: Col. C. Carroll Marsh
11th Illinois • 20th Illinois • 45th Illinois • 48th Illinois

Third Brigade: Col. Julius Raith (mw); Lt. Col. Enos P. Wood
17th Illinois • 29th Illinois • 43rd Illinois • 49th Illinois

Unattached
Dresser's 2nd Illinois Light Artillery, Battery D • McAllister's 1st Illinois Light Artillery   Battery D
Schwartz's 2nd Illinois Light Artillery, Battery E • Burrows 14th Ohio Light Artillery
4th Illinois Cavalry, 1st Battalion • Carmichael's Company, Illinois Cavalry • Stewart's Company, Illinois Cavalry

SECOND DIVISION: Brig. Gen. William H. L. Wallace (mw); Col. James M. Tuttle
First Brigade: Col. James M. Tuttle
2nd Iowa • 7th Iowa • 12th Iowa • 14th Iowa

Second Brigade: Brig. Gen. John McArthur (w); Col. Thomas Morton
9th Illinois • 12th Illinois • 13th Missouri • 14th Missouri • 81st Ohio

Third Brigade: Col. Thomas W. Sweeny (w); Col. Silas D. Baldwin
8th Iowa • 7th Illinois • 50th Illinois • 52nd Illinois • 57th Illinois • 58th Illinois

Artillery
Willard's 1st Illinois Light Artillery, Battery A • Cavender's Battalion, Missouri Artillery
Richardson's 1st Missouri Light Artillery, Battery D • Welker's 1st Missouri Light Artillery, Battery H
Stone's 1st Missouri Light Artillery, Battery K

Cavalry
2nd Illinois Cavalry, Company A • 2nd Illinois Cavalry, Company B • 2nd U.S. Cavalry, Company C
4th U.S. Cavalry, Company I

THIRD DIVISION: Maj. Gen. Lew Wallace
First Brigade: Col. Morgan L. Smith
11th Indiana • 24th Indiana • 8th Missouri

Second Brigade: Col. John M. Thayer
23rd Indiana • 1st Nebraska • 58th Ohio • 68th Ohio

Third Brigade: Col. Charles Whittlesey
20th Ohio • 56th Ohio • 76th Ohio • 78th Ohio

Artillery
Thompson's 9th Indiana Light Artillery • Buell's 1st Missouri Light Artillery, Battery I

Cavalry
11th Illinois Cavalry, 3rd Battalion • 5th Ohio Cavalry, 3rd Battalion

FOURTH DIVISION: Brig. Gen. Stephen A. Hurlbut
First Brigade: Col. Nelson G. Williams (d); Col. Isaac C. Pugh
28th Illinois • 32nd Illinois • 41st Illinois • 3rd Iowa

Second Brigade: Col. James C. Veatch
14th Illinois • 15th Illinois • 46th Illinois • 25th Indiana

Third Brigade: Brig. Gen. Jacob G. Lauman
31st Indiana • 44th Indiana • 17th Kentucky • 25th Kentucky

Artillery
Ross's 2nd Michigan Light Artillery • Mann's 1st Missouri Light Artillery, Battery C
Myers's 13th Ohio Light Artillery

Cavalry
5th Ohio Cavalry, 1st and 2nd Battalions

FIFTH DIVISION: Brig. Gen. William T. Sherman (w)
First Brigade: Col. John A. McDowell
40th Illinois • 6th Iowa • 46th Ohio

Second Brigade: Col. David Stuart (w); Lt. Col. Oscar Malmborg; Col. T. Kilby Smith
55th Illinois • 54th Ohio • 71st Ohio

Third Brigade: Col. Jesse Hildebrand
53rd Ohio • 57th Ohio • 77th Ohio

Fourth Brigade: Col. Ralph P. Buckland
48th Ohio • 70th Ohio • 72nd Ohio

Artillery: Maj. Ezra Taylor
Barrett's 1st Illinois Light Artillery Battery B • Waterhouse's 1st Illinois Light Artillery Battery E
Morton's 6th Indiana Light Artillery

Cavalry
4th Illinois Cavalry, 2nd and 3rd Battalions • Thielemann's two companies, Illinois Cavalry

SIXTH DIVISION: Brig. Gen. Benjamin M. Prentiss (c)
First Brigade: Col. Everett Peabody
12th Michigan • 21st Missouri • 25th Missouri • 16th Wisconsin

Second Brigade: Col. Madison Miller (c)
61st Illinois • 18th Missouri • 18th Wisconsin

Unattached
15th Iowa • 16th Iowa • 23rd Missouri

Artillery
Hickenlooper's 5th Ohio Light Artillery • Munch's 1st Minnesota Light Artillery

Cavalry
11th Illinois Cavalry, 1st and 2nd Battalions

Unattached
15th Michigan • 14th Wisconsin • Silfversparre's 1st Illinois Light Artillery Battery H
Bouton's 1st Illinois Light Artillery, Battery I • Madison's 2nd Illinois Artillery, Battery B
Powell's 2nd Illinois Light Artillery, Battery F • Markgraf's 8th Ohio Light Artillery

ARMY OF THE OHIO
Maj. Gen. Don Carlos Buell

SECOND DIVISION: Brig. Gen. Alexander McCook
Fourth Brigade: Brig. Gen. Lovell Rousseau
6th Indiana; 5th Kentucky; 1st Ohio; 15th U.S., 1st Battalion • 16th U.S.,
1st Battalion • 19th U.S., 1st Battalion

Fifth Brigade: Col. Edward N. Kirk (w)
34th Illinois • 29th Indiana • 30th Indiana • 77th Pennsylvania

Sixth Brigade: Col. William H. Gibson
32nd Indiana • 39th Indiana • 15th Ohio • 49th Ohio

Artillery
Terrill's 5th U.S., Battery H

FOURTH DIVISION: Brig. Gen. William Nelson
Tenth Brigade: Col. Jacob Ammen
36th Indiana • 6th Ohio • 24th Ohio

Nineteenth Brigade: Col. William B. Hazen
9th Indiana • 6th Kentucky • 41st Ohio

Twenty-second Brigade: Col. Sanders D. Bruce
1st Kentucky • 2nd Kentucky • 20th Kentucky

FIFTH DIVISION: Brig. Gen. Thomas L. Crittenden
Eleventh Brigade: Brig. Gen. Jeremiah T. Boyle
9th Kentucky • 13th Kentucky • 19th Ohio • 59th Ohio

Fourteenth Brigade: Col. William Sooy Smith
11th Kentucky • 26th Kentucky • 13th Ohio

Artillery
Bartlett's 1st Ohio Light Artillery, Battery G • Mendenhall's 4th U.S. Artillery, Batteries H & M

SIXTH DIVISION: Brig. Gen. Thomas J. Wood
Twentieth Brigade: Brig. Gen. James A. Garfield
13th Michigan • 64th Ohio • 65th Ohio

Twenty-first Brigade: Col. George D. Wagner
15th Indiana • 40th Indiana • 57th Indiana • 24th Kentucky

* * *

ARMY OF THE MISSISSIPPI
Gen. Albert Sidney Johnston (k)
Gen. P. G. T. Beauregard

FIRST ARMY CORPS: Maj. Gen. Leonidas Polk
FIRST DIVISION: Brig. Gen. Charles Clark (w); Brig. Gen. Alexander P. Stewart
First Brigade: Col. Robert M. Russell
11th Louisiana • 12th Tennessee • 13th Tennessee • 22nd Tennessee • Bankhead's Tennessee Battery

Second Brigade: Brig. Gen. Alexander P. Stewart
13th Arkansas • 4th Tennessee • 5th Tennessee • 33rd Tennessee • Stanford's Mississippi Battery

SECOND DIVISION: Brig. Gen. Benjamin F. Cheatham (w)
First Brigade: Brig. Gen. Bushrod Johnson (w); Col. Preston Smith (w)
Blythe's Mississippi Regiment • 2nd Tennessee • 15th Tennessee • 154th Tennessee • Polk's Tennessee Battery

Second Brigade: Col. William H. Stephens; Col. George Maney
7th Kentucky • 1st Tennessee Battalion • 6th Tennessee • 9th Tennessee • Smith's Mississippi Battery

Cavalry
1st Mississippi Cavalry • Brewer's Mississippi and Alabama Battalion

Unattached
47th Tennessee

SECOND ARMY CORPS: Maj. Gen. Braxton Bragg
FIRST DIVISION: Brig. Gen. Daniel Ruggles
First Brigade: Col. Randall L. Gibson
1st Arkansas • 4th Louisiana • 13th Louisiana • 19th Louisiana

Second Brigade: Brig. Gen. Patton Anderson
1st Florida Battalion • 17th Louisiana • 20th Louisiana • Confederate Guards Response Battalion
9th Texas • Washington (Louisiana) Artillery, 5th Company

Third Brigade: Col. Preston Pond, Jr.
16th Louisiana • 18th Louisiana • Crescent (Louisiana) Regiment • Orleans Guard (Louisiana) Battalion
38th Tennessee • Ketchum's Alabama Battery

Cavalry
Jenkins's Alabama Battalion of five companies

SECOND DIVISION: Brig. Gen. Jones M. Withers
First Brigade: Brig. Gen. Adley H. Gladden (mw); Col. Daniel W. Adams (w);
Col. Zach C. Deas (w)
21st Alabama • 22nd Alabama • 25th Alabama • 26th Alabama • 1st Louisiana

Robertson's Florida Battery

Second Brigade: Brig. Gen. James R. Chalmers
5th Mississippi • 7th Mississippi • 9th Mississippi • 10th Mississippi • 52nd Tennessee
Gage's Alabama Battery

Third Brigade: Brig. Gen. John K. Jackson
17th Alabama • 18th Alabama • 19th Alabama • 2nd Texas • Girardey's Georgia Battery (Washington Artillery)

Cavalry
Clanton's Alabama Regiment

THIRD ARMY CORPS: Maj. Gen. William J. Hardee (w)
First Brigade: Brig. Gen. Thomas C. Hindman (d); Col. R. G. Shaver (d)
2nd Arkansas • 6th Arkansas • 7th Arkansas • 3rd Confederate • Warren Light Artillery
Pillow Flying Artillery (or Miller's Tennessee Battery)

Second Brigade: Brig. Gen. Patrick R. Cleburne
15th Arkansas • 6th Mississippi • 2nd Tennessee • 5th (35th) Tennessee • 23rd Tennessee • 24th Tennessee
Shoup's Artillery Battalion: Trigg's (Austin) Arkansas Battery • Calvert's (Helena) Arkansas Light Artillery
Hubbard's Arkansas Battery

Third Brigade: Brig. Gen. Sterling A. M. Wood (d); Col. William K. Patterson
16th Alabama • 8th Arkansas • 9th (14th) Arkansas Battalion • 3rd Mississippi Battalion
27th Tennessee • 44th Tennessee • 55th Tennessee • Jefferson Mississippi Flying Artillery • Georgia Dragoons

RESERVE CORPS: Brig. Gen. John C. Breckinridge
First Brigade: Col. Robert P. Trabue
Clifton's 4th Alabama Battalion • 31st Alabama • 3rd Kentucky • 4th Kentucky • 5th Kentucky
6th Kentucky • Crew's Tennessee Battalion • Cobb's Kentucky Battery • Byrne's Kentucky Battery
Morgan's Squadron Kentucky Cavalry

Second Brigade: Brig. Gen. John S. Bowen (w); Col. John D. Martin
9th Arkansas • 10th Arkansas • 2nd Confederate • 1st Missouri • Pettus Mississippi Flying Artillery
Watson Louisiana Flying Artillery • Thompson's Company Kentucky Cavalry

Third Brigade: Col. Winfield S. Statham
15th Mississippi • 22nd Mississippi • 19th Tennessee • 20th Tennessee • 28th Tennessee
45th Tennessee • Rutledge's Tennessee Battery

Unattached
Forrest's Regiment Tennessee Cavalry • Wharton's Texas Regiment Cavalry
Wirt Adams's Mississippi Regiment Cavalry • McClung's Tennessee Battery • Roberts's Arkansas Battery

Suggested Reading

THE BATTLE OF SHILOH

Shiloh: Blue & Gray Magazine Civil War Sesquicentennial Edition
Stacy D. Allen
Blue & Gray Enterprises (2010)
ISBN: 1-891515-04-7

Stacy Allen has dedicated his career to the interpretation, preservation, and protection of Shiloh National Military Park. No reading list about Shiloh would be complete without sources providing his views on the relative importance of the Sunken Road and other aspects affecting our understanding of the battle.

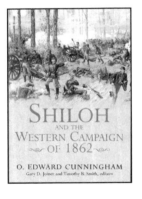

Shiloh and the Western Campaign of 1862
O. Edward Cunningham (edited by Gary D. Joiner and Timothy B. Smith)
Savas Beatie (2007)
ISBN-13: 978-1-932714-27-2

This previously unpublished, 40-year-old manuscript was so highly regarded by those familiar with it that a team of historians felt it needed to appear in print and be shared with the public. The editors' footnotes contribute greatly to an understanding of some of the differing interpretations of the battle.

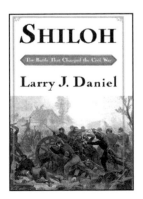

Shiloh: The Battle that Changed the Civil War
Larry J. Daniel
Simon & Schuster (1997)
ISBN: 0-684-80375-5

This well-written and easy-reading book is organized by location, so readers who think spatially and like to know where events took place will particularly enjoy the way in which the book is laid out.

Confederates in the Attic
Tony Horwitz
Pantheon Books (1998)
ISBN: 0-679-43978-1

Chapter 8 in *Confederates in the Attic* dramatically helps anyone to understand the battlefield as it exists today, especially if they first visited Shiloh several decades ago.

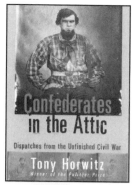

Shiloh—in Hell before Night
James Lee McDonough
University of Tennessee Press (1977)
ISBN: 0-87049-232-2

A unique aspect of this volume is that it offers the most critical assessment of the leadership of A. S. Johnston among the various books on Shiloh.

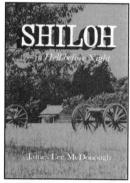

Shiloh: Conquer or Perish
Timothy B. Smith
University of Kansas Press (2014)
ISBN-13: 978-0-7006-1995-5

The term "definitive" should be used sparingly, but this well-researched and well-written study will serve as the definitive book on Shiloh for decades. Tim Smith is the most prolific author of works about Shiloh, including the battles fought just before and after Shiloh, as well as the history of the park. Also, highly recommended are his two books of essays on Shiloh: *The Untold Story of Shiloh* and *Rethinking Shiloh*.

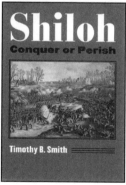

Shiloh: Bloody April
Wiley Sword
Morningside (1983; Revised Edition 2001)
ISBN-13: 978-0-8902-9070-5

Wiley Sword wrote the first detailed book on the battle; it will forever be the classic volume about Shiloh, upon which all other books have built. Among the unique aspects of his work, in the revised 2001 edition, Sword offers an interpretation about where A. S. Johnston was wounded that differs from the traditional location.

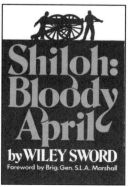

About the Author

Gregory A. Mertz is a native of what is now Wildwood, Missouri. He is an Eagle Scout, belonging to Boy Scout Troop 782, which visited Shiloh National Military Park to hike and camp each spring. Greg hiked each of the six scout trails at Shiloh, totaling 88 miles and completing the requirements to earn the Shiloh Veteran Hiker Award.

He graduated from the University of Missouri with a bachelor's degree in Recreation and Park Administration and from Shippensburg University with a master's degree in Public Administration.

Greg has worked for the National Park Service for more than 37 years, holding positions at Gettysburg National Military Park, Eisenhower National Historic Site, and Fredericksburg and Spotsylvania National Military Park. As the supervisory historian for more than two decades at Fredericksburg, he has trained hundreds of seasonal employees, interns, and volunteers in informal interpretation and the conducting of interpretive programs.

He was the charter president of the Rappahannock Valley Civil War Round Table and was the vice president of the Brandy Station Foundation preservation group.

Greg frequently speaks to Civil War roundtables on a variety of Civil War subjects. He has written four feature articles for *Blue and Gray Magazine* on the battles of the Wilderness and Spotsylvania Court House.

During the Sesquicentennial of the Civil War, Greg gave anniversary tours at First Manassas, Cedar Mountain, Antietam, Fredericksburg, Chancellorsville, Gettysburg, Wilderness, Spotsylvania Court House, and Cedar Creek. On other occasions, he has also given tours of Kelly's Ford, Brandy Station, Bristoe Station, Rappahannock Station, and Mine Run.